INVITATION TO THE BOOK OF REVELATION

This volume continues a series of commentaries on the books of the Bible, specially designed to answer the need for a lively, contemporary guide to the written Word. Here is the best of contemporary biblical scholarship, together with the world-renowned *Jerusalem Bible* text. In addition, there are study questions that will provoke and inspire further discussion.

The Book of Revelation has fascinated people down through the ages. It is one of the finest examples of apocalyptic literature that speaks prophetically of the past, the present, and the future in mythological language and images. It tells what might happen unless the world repents of its sins. Authors have spent almost two thousand years trying to decipher the Book of Revelation, and its treasures are still weaving their spell. One thing can be said: The Book of Revelation is a call for repentance and renewal just as important today as it was for the early Christian world.

INVITATION TO THE BOOK OF REVELATION presents this Book and its message in a format that can be easily used for individual study, daily meditation, and/or group discussion. It is an indispensable volume for any Christian library.

INVITATION TO THE
BOOK OF REVELATION

INVITATION TO THE BOOK OF REVELATION

*A Commentary on the Apocalypse
with Complete Text
from The Jerusalem Bible*

ELISABETH SCHÜSSLER FIORENZA

IMAGE BOOKS
A Division of Doubleday & Company, Inc.
Garden City, New York
1981

In memory of

Elisabeth Käsemann
Archbishop O. Romero
Karen Silkwood
Steve Biko

Who have died in their struggle for justice

The text of the Book of Revelation is from The Jerusalem Bible, copyright © 1966 by Darton, Longman & Todd, Ltd., and Doubleday & Company, Inc. Used by permission of the publisher.

ISBN: 0-385-14800-3
Library of Congress Catalog Card Number: 79-6744

Commentary Copyright © 1981 by
Elisabeth Schüssler Fiorenza
General Introduction Copyright © 1977 by
Robert J. Karris
All Rights Reserved
Printed in the United States of America
First Edition

CONTENTS

ABBREVIATIONS OF THE BOOKS OF THE BIBLE

Ac	Acts	Lk	Luke
Am	Amos	Lm	Lamentations
Ba	Baruch	Lv	Leviticus
1 Ch	1 Chronicles	1 M	1 Maccabees
2 Ch	2 Chronicles	2 M	2 Maccabees
1 Co	1 Corinthians	Mi	Micah
2 Co	2 Corinthians	Mk	Mark
Col	Colossians	Ml	Malachi
Dn	Daniel	Mt	Matthew
Dt	Deuteronomy	Na	Nahum
Ep	Ephesians	Nb	Numbers
Est	Esther	Ne	Nehemiah
Ex	Exodus	Ob	Obadiah
Ezk	Ezekiel	1 P	1 Peter
Ezr	Ezra	2 P	2 Peter
Ga	Galatians	Ph	Philippians
Gn	Genesis	Phm	Philemon
Hab	Habakkuk	Pr	Proverbs
Heb	Hebrews	Ps	Psalms
Hg	Haggai	Qo	Ecclesiastes
Ho	Hosea	Rm	Romans
Is	Isaiah	Rt	Ruth
Jb	Job	Rv	Revelation
Jdt	Judith	1 S	1 Samuel
Jg	Judges	2 S	2 Samuel
Jl	Joel	Sg	Song of Songs
Jm	James	Si	Ecclesiasticus
Jn	John	Tb	Tobit
1 Jn	1 John	1 Th	1 Thessalonians
2 Jn	2 John	2 Th	2 Thessalonians
3 Jn	3 John	1 Tm	1 Timothy
Jon	Jonah	2 Tm	2 Timothy
Jos	Joshua	Tt	Titus
Jr	Jeremiah	Ws	Wisdom
Jude	Jude	Zc	Zechariah
1 K	1 Kings	Zp	Zephaniah
2 K	2 Kings		

GENERAL INTRODUCTION TO THE DOUBLEDAY NEW TESTAMENT COMMENTARY SERIES

Let me introduce this new commentary series on the New Testament by sharing some experiences. In my job as New Testament Book Review Editor for the *Catholic Biblical Quarterly,* scores of books pass through my hands each year. As I evaluate these books and send them out to reviewers, I cannot help but think that so little of this scholarly research will make its way into the hands of the educated lay person.

In talking at biblical institutes and to charismatic and lay study groups, I find an almost unquenchable thirst for the Word of God. People want to learn more; they want to study. But when they ask me to recommend commentaries on the New Testament, I'm stumped. What commentaries can I put into their hands, commentaries that do not have the technical jargon of scholars and that really communicate to the educated laity?

The goal of this popular commentary series is to make the best of contemporary scholarship available to the educated lay person in a highly readable and understandable way. The commentaries avoid footnotes and other scholarly apparatus. They are short and sweet. The authors make their points in a clear way and don't fatigue their readers with unnecessary detail.

Another outstanding feature of this commentary

series is that it is based on The Jerusalem Bible translation, which is serialized with the commentary. This lively and easily understandable translation has received rave reviews from millions of readers. It is the interstate of translations and avoids the stoplights of local-road translations.

A signal feature of the commentaries on the Gospels is that they explore the way each evangelist used the sayings and deeds of Jesus to meet the needs of his church. The commentators answer the question: How did each evangelist guide, challenge, teach, and console the members of his community with the message of Jesus? The commentators are not interested in the evangelist's message for its own sake, but explain that message with one eye on present application.

This last-mentioned feature goes hand and glove with the innovative feature of appending Study Questions to the explanations of individual passages. By means of these Study Questions the commentator moves from an explanation of the message of the evangelist to a consideration of how this message might apply to believers today.

Each commentator has two highly important qualifications: scholarly expertise and the proven ability to communicate the results of solid scholarship to the people of God.

I am confident that this new commentary series will meet a real need as it helps people to unlock a door to the storehouse of God's Word where they will find food for life.

ROBERT J. KARRIS, O.F.M.
Associate Professor of New Testament Studies,
Catholic Theological Union and
Chicago Cluster of Theological Schools

PREFACE

At the time when I was revising parts of this commentary, the archbishop of El Salvador, Oscar Romero, was assassinated. His violent death called to mind the names of other victims who were killed in their quest and struggle for justice: The German student Elisabeth Käsemann, who was killed in Argentina; the American union worker Karen Silkwood, whose fatal accident ended her struggle for a safe and healthy workplace; the South African student leader Steve Biko, who died from brain injury sustained while in detention. They, like Romero and many others whose names are not known or forgotten, are the victims of contemporary oppressive political powers and regimes. As in John's time so too today the blood of those murdered unjustly cries out for justice and liberation. This commentary of Revelation is dedicated to the memory of their suffering and struggle.

Feminist theology has pointed out how much androcentric language perpetuates the deep alienation and subtle oppression of women in religion. I have, therefore, sought to avoid such androcentric language whenever possible. Since I was, however, not able to change the androcentric translation of the biblical text itself, I apologize to all those who are offended by such androcentric language.

Finally, I want to thank my students at Notre Dame, St. John's in Collegeville, and Union Theological Seminary in New York whose critical and challenging questions have helped me to deepen my own theological interpretation of Revelation.

INVITATION TO THE
BOOK OF REVELATION

INTRODUCTION

The Book of Revelation remains for many Christians a book with seven seals, seldom read and relegated to a curiosity in the Bible. For others it has become *the* book of the New Testament, full of information about the present situation and full of predictions for what is to come in the future. Many Christians view their present situation and the future ahead through Revelation's lenses. Such books as Hal Lindsey's *The Late, Great Planet Earth,* which provide detailed application of the book's visions to contemporary events, enjoy widespread popularity. Throughout history Christians have maintained that, e.g., the beast symbolizes such contemporary personalities as the pope in Rome, Hitler or Stalin, or more recently the leaders of Islam who are against the American people. A few years ago when West Germany attempted to work out a treaty with the U.S.S.R., a fundamentalist radio station informed its listeners that the West German chancellor was the second beast and anti-Christ.

Historical-critical scholarship is also very uneasy about the book because its theology is suspect and its bizarre images elude any logical-rational reduction. Scholars generally agree that the book should be understood in the context of the first century and the cultural ambience of its first readers. However, they often claim that the book is more Jewish than Christian and far below the theological level of Paul or John. As so-called apocalyptic literature, it is only slightly Christianized and contributes little to our understanding of early Christian life and theology.

Symbolic Language and Mythological Imagery

Although Revelation's classification as apocalyptic literature is correct, such a classification should be understood not so much as a theological evaluation but as a literary circumscription. Jewish apocalyptic literature speaks about the past, present, and future in mythological language and images. For example, Daniel has a vision of four wild beasts emerging from the sea that are later identified as four great kings (cf. ch. 7). The bizarre and terrifying features of these beasts indicate that they are not conceived as real beasts but as mythological symbolizations. The first beast, for instance, is likened to a lion with eagle's wings, while the third is compared to a leopard with four heads and four bird wings on its flanks (Dn 7:4–7). Thus in apocalyptic literature, world empires have become beasts, nations are symbolized by birds, and serpents start to speak. At the same time, apocalyptic authors describe the future in terms of the knowledge available to them and speak about heavenly or demonic realities that are not available to common human experience and knowledge in human language and imagery derived from the mythology, traditions, and scientific knowledge of their time. Therefore, apocalyptic literature could be compared with the future-oriented genre of science fiction that constructs the future out of the experience and fears of people in the present. Anyone enjoying the tales and future projections of science fiction writings, however, would readily agree that this literature illuminates our present situation and projects our hopes and fears for the future.

Revelation's classification as apocalyptic literature therefore signals that its images and visions should not be understood in terms of historical description nor in terms of future prediction. The author who in 1:1 identifies himself as John has not much more information about the endtime than do the authors of the Synoptic apocalypse Mark 13 parallels or 1 Thessalonians 4:13 ff, 1 Corinthians 15:20 ff, or 2 Thessalonians 2:1 ff. However, the dramatic presentation elaborates these early Christian expectations with the help of traditional language and contemporary images. As does all science fiction, so apocalyptic literature in general and Revelation in particular seek to make sense of the world and present time in terms of the future or of the transcendent. At the same time it pictures the future with the help of knowledge and language gleaned from the past and the present.

However, Revelation is not written for the sake of entertainment, esoteric knowledge, or for future prediction but for the sake of prophetic interpretation and motivation. As a Christian prophet, the author does not just give injunctions and admonitions but constructs a symbolic universe and "plausibility structure" in order to make sense out of the experience of Christians who believe that the ultimate sources of political power are God and Christ, but experience daily poverty, persecution, and execution. John portrays this experience and predicament of Christians who are powerless in terms of the political powers of the time. Therefore, he expresses his vision of the Christian symbolic universe in socio-economic language and political-mythological imagery. In creating this mythological symbolization he

does not freely create his metaphors and language but
derives them from Jewish and Greco-Roman literature
and tradition. In working with associations and allusions to very divergent mythic and religious-political
traditions, he appeals to the imagination of people
steeped in Jewish and Hellenistic culture and religion.

John achieves the literary-symbolic power of his
work by taking his traditional images and mythological
symbols out of their original context and by placing
them like mosaic stones into a new literary composition
and mythological symbolization. Therefore, Revelation
must be heard and contemplated as a symphony of images and symbols if one wants to experience its full
emotional and symbolic impact. Literary and historical
analyses can deepen this experience but not replace it.
An analysis of Revelation's sources and traditions
helps to elucidate the possible meaning of its images
but such an analysis does not "explain" the book.
Their meaning cannot be derived from the tradition but
only from their present position within the overall
framework and narrative flow of the book.

The strength of Revelation's language and images
lies not in theological argumentation or historical information but in their evocative power inviting imaginative participation. The symbolization and narrative
movement of Revelation elicit emotions, feelings, and
convictions that cannot, and should not, be fully con-
ceptualized. The phrasing of the images and metaphors
in propositional, logical, factual language robs them of
their power of persuasion. The mythopoetic language
of Revelation is akin to poetry and drama. Therefore,
any adequate exploration and comprehension of Revelation has to experience the evocative power and "mu-
sicality" of the book's language since it was written to

be read aloud as a liturgical poem and to be heard in the worship gatherings of the Asian communities.

Although scholars had acknowledged by the eighteenth century that apocalyptic language is poetic language and that even in antiquity prophecy was considered similar to poetry, they nevertheless have attempted to relegate apocalyptic language to mere form from which the historical or theological content can be distilled. They have reduced mythological symbolization to timeless principles or ontological archetypes, since the often bizarre imagery or crude mythology offends rational-logical sensibilities. Such an interpretative tendency is also provoked by the theological evaluation of Revelation as a myth of revenge and a drama of resentment which is deemed incompatible with a Christian theology of love and forgiveness.

However, if apocalyptic language is akin to poetry then we should approach Revelation as we would read a poem. The following poem of a contemporary poet may illustrate what I have in mind.

Exodus

Out of cattle pen tenements
where the will to live fades out
like a forty watt bulb in the hallway's crotch;
out of streets rampant with proud metal
where men are mice at work
and slavering dogs afterward;
out of beds where women offer up
their only part prized whose name
is an insult and means woman here;
where anxiety yellows the air;

where greed paints over every window;
where defeat private as a worm
gnaws every belly,
we begin our slow halting exodus.
Egypt, you formed me from your clay.
I am a doll baked in your factory ovens,
yet I have risen and walked.

Like the Golem I am makeshift, lumbering.
I rattle and wheeze and my parts
are cannibalized T-birds and sewing machines,
mixers and wheelchairs, hair dryers.
My skin is the papier-mâché of newspapers
cured with the tears of children
pregnant with hunger. My heart
is the stolen engine of an F-111.
My ligaments are knitting needles, hangers
recovered from the bodies of
self-aborted women. My teeth are military
headstones. I am the Golem.
Many breathed rage and hope into my
lungs, their roar
is my voice, their dreams
burning are my fuel.
They say nothing but a desert stretches
beyond, where the skulls of visionaries
are scoured by ants.

We have entered our Thirty Years' War
for a green place called the Country
of the Living. For two generations
we will be walking to a land we must build,

ourselves the bricks, the boards, the bridges,
in every face the map,
in every hand the highway.
We go clanking, stumbling forward, lurching.
Children born in that country
will play in the wreckage of our fears.

Marge Piercy, *The Twelve-Spoked Wheel Flashing*, New York: A. Knopf, 1978, pp. 31–32.

It is obvious that it is helpful, but not necessary, for understanding this poem to explain what the literal meaning of expressions as "exodus," "Egypt," or "Golem" is. People who have never seen an F-111 or hair dryers and mixers might be helped by an explanation of these technological gadgets. Yet all such information would not allow them to grasp the meaning of the poem.

More important than the explanation of certain terms is the delineation of the cultural context and critique that provides the framework of the poem and interconnects its language with people and events of a certain culture and time. The context of the poem is obviously a critical analysis of technological society and especially a feminist analysis of the image and situation of women in such a society. Anyone who has never read a critique of how the media present women and how advertising makes objects of women will have a difficult time in identifying with the poem. Anyone who has not explored sexual oppression will react in a prudish way or not understand why the biblical images of Exodus and Egypt symbolize the women's movement.

It is obvious that an attempt to solve the problem of how the teeth of the poet can be likened to "military

headstones" or the location of the desert where "the
skulls of visionaries are scoured by ants" must fail by
definition. Similarly, ridiculous would be a claim that
the poet predicts that the struggle of the women's
movement will last thirty years and that the children playing "in the wreckage of our fears" will actually be our grandchildren.

However, the meaning of the poem is also lost when
its cultural-societal context is lost. To claim that the
poem speaks about the archetypal domination of
women by men, or the timeless yearning of people for
the "golden age," or about the predicament of the
human situation in all ages is to overlook the evocative
and emotive power of its images in a certain situation
based on an experience shared with the audience.

While the poem of Marge Piercy belongs to a collection of poems which are only loosely related to each
other, Revelation's "poetic" visions are set within an
overall framework of an apocalyptic myth. The expression "mythological symbolization" defines Revelation
as a cohesive body of images and symbols constituting
an apocalyptic myth that has its meaning in itself.
Therefore, the mythological symbolization of Revelation can be broken down into its component symbols
and images on the one hand and on the other hand the
individual images or metaphors can be understood only
within the overall literary composition and dramatic
structure of the book.

Literary Composition and Structure

Therefore, Revelation can be fully understood only
when analyzed as a literary composition because each
vision and symbol takes its import in its relation to the
overall architecture of the work. Although the author

mixes together traditional symbols and patterns of very
disparate origin, Revelation makes a very unified and
well-organized impression in comparison to other
apocalypses. That Revelation is not encyclopedic but
dramatic in character is due to the author's literary
techniques and compositional skills that integrate the
various traditions and symbols into the literary movement of the work.

A primary means to achieve a unified composition is
his use of a *common stock of symbols and images*. The
individual visions of the book do not have an exclusive
set of images that are found nowhere else in the book.
To the contrary, the main symbols and images are distributed over the whole work, e.g., the symbol of the
throne or the image of *prostration*. The author also
achieves a unified narrative structure by employing
image clusters and symbol associations that re-enforce
each other and, like a musical motif, connect the individual visions with each other (e.g., the image of the
throne achieves its full impact and "volume" by its allusions and associations with other symbols of imperial
power and reign). Further techniques of literary integration are *preannouncements* (e.g., the promises to
the victor at the end of the seven messages is developed
in ch. 21 f), *cross-references* (Christological characteristics of the inaugural vision are repeated not only in
ch. 2 f but also in 14:14 ff and 19:11 ff), and *contrasts* (e.g., the great Babylon in ch. 17 f and the New
Jerusalem of chs. 12 and 21 f).

A primary means for achieving an interwoven tex-
ture and unified composition is the author's use of
numbers and numerical patterns. Basic numerical-
structural component forms are the four "seven cycles"
of the messages and plagues, the two book visions
which symbolize a new prophetic commissioning, and

the two visions of Christ with the sword, the symbol of
judgment (cf. 1:13 ff; 19:11 ff). The seven cycles in
turn are again structured into four and three groupings.
This numerical interweaving of visions has the effect of
combining a cyclic form of repetition with a continuous
forward movement, which characterizes Revelation as
end-oriented rather than cyclic or encyclopedic. The
forward surge of the narrative is interpreted through
interludes that are generally visions of eschatological
protection and salvation. Insofar as the author interrupts the patterns of continuous narrative and cyclic
repetition through the insertion of these anticipatory visions of salvation, he underlines the interrelation between the present situation of oppression and the eschatological future of salvation. At the same time he
maintains structurally that the eschatological future
gives meaning to the present situation and struggle.

Very important for the understanding of Revelation
are the literary techniques of intercalation and of interlocking that make a diagramming of the successive
sections and development of Revelation almost impossible. The method of intercalation, or sandwiching, is
used by the author in the following way. He narrates
two episodes or uses two symbols or images which essentially belong together. Between these two sections or
symbols (A and A'), he then intercalates another (B)
and thus requires the reader to see the whole text as an
indivisible whole. For example, the seven-trumpet
series is introduced by the following inclusion:

A: Next I saw seven trumpets being given. . . . (8:2)
B: Another angel who had a golden censer. . . .
(8:3–5)
A': The seven angels that had the seven trumpets. . . . (8:6 ff)

Thus many sections of Revelation are structured in the form of an inclusion.

The technique of interlocking or interlacing is a combination of the ABA' pattern and the interlude. The author inserts into the preceding passage a section or vision which clearly belongs also to the following section (e.g., the section 10:1–11:14 is an interlude before the opening of the seventh trumpet and at the same time is clearly characterized as a part of chs. 12–14). The method of intercalation represents the greatest obstacle to our Western minds because we are trained to divide a text into sections that follow each other in a logical-linear fashion. The author of Revelation, however, does not *separate* the narrative structure into clear-cut segments or logical sequences but seeks to *join* the individual visions and cycles together by interweaving them with each other through the techniques of intercalation and inclusion. Although scholars usually look for the "dividing marks" of Revelation, it seems to me more fruitful to concentrate on the *joints* that interlink the different cycles of visions with each other.

One can almost find as many outlines and structurations of Revelation as there are scholars studying the book. Since we are trained in linear-logical thinking we expect a linear-temporal sequence of visions. Therefore, we are startled by anticipatory interludes and hymns, apparent repetitions, and the repeated announcement that the end is here. Nevertheless, Revelation is not cyclic since its narrative moves forward. Insofar as the promises of the seven messages all recur in the last section of the book, this forward movement is a movement from promise to fulfillment. Yet this forward movement of the narrative is not linear-logical or linear-temporal. It can best be envisioned as a conic spiral moving from the present to the eschatological future. However, this forward movement of the narrative is not a flight into a utopian future but is anchored in the present of the communities. The total literary vision of Revelation is set within the epistolary framework of an open pastoral-prophetic letter, on the one hand, and exhortations, beatitudes, and warnings referring the apocalyptic images and visions to the present experience of the Christian community, on the other hand.

The outline or structure of Revelation is determined by the forward movement of the narrative as well as by the concentric pattern of the epistolary inclusion. Its individual elements can be sketched in the following way:

A. 1:1–8: Epistolary frame and prologue
B. 1:9–3:22: First seven cycle
C. 4:1–9:21; 11:15–19: Second and third seven cycles
D. 10:1–15:4: The "little" scroll
C'. 15:1–19:10: Fourth seven cycle
B'. 19:11–22:9: Eschatological visions
A'. 22:10–22:21: Epistolary frame and epilogue
(For a more developed outline, see Appendix.)

This concentric ABCDC'B'A' structure is found also in Jewish and Greco-Roman literature and art. It indicates that the whole book is conceived as an inclusion (see Glossary) that could be compared to the several layers of an onion.

However, Revelation's narrative is not static but dynamic. It can best be envisioned as a concentric spiral moving from the present to the eschatological future. Its development of symbol and thought is not chrono-

logical but topical or thematical. It could be likened to
that of a dramatic motion picture whose individual
scenes portray the persons or action every time from a
different angle or perspective while at the same time
adding some new insight to the whole. It also could be
likened to a musical composition that varies the musical themes in different ways, each variation enhancing
and moving the total composition. In my opinion,
Sonia Delaunay's expressionist paintings visualize best
the development of symbol and movement in Revelation. Her picture "rhythm," for instance, contains a
number of different-colored circles or half circles from
which radiate lines of colors like light that seems to
be splintered by a prism. The picture is not static, but
its lines indicate a forward movement of the circles
of color like a revolving planet. While the evolving
circles of color suggest simultaneity, the contrasting
colors create a sense of light and movement.

We have to keep in mind, however, that John does
not develop such a dynamic composition for art's sake
but for the sake of prophetic motivation and interpretation. The symbolic universe or literary vision con-
structed by the author seeks to give theological meaning to the experience of Christians in Asia Minor at the
end of the first century. John receives his inspiration
not from the muses but from the prophetic Spirit. At
the same time he shares the ambition of Jewish apocalypticism to create a literary vision instead of a sermon
or tract.

Theological Perspective

The major theological motifs of Revelation are those
of power and justice. The central theological symbol of
the book is the throne signifying divine or demonic

power. While the Christians are the representatives and agents of the power and empire of God and Christ here on earth, the universal Roman empire and its imperial powers are the agents of the demonic and destructive power of Satan. Revelation is thus a deeply political-theological book.

Like John, Christians of Asia Minor suffered a deep tension between their faith and their experience. They believed in the ultimate power of God and Christ, but at the same time they experienced daily their powerlessness in the face of harassment, oppression, and persecution. Their everyday experiences ran counter to their belief in God's power and undermined their hope in God's empire, glory, and life-giving power. This tension between faith conviction and negative experience in everyday life provoked difficult theological questions: If God and Christ have the real power in the world, why do their loyal believers have to suffer? Why does Christ not return in glory and without delay to prevent further suffering and to adjudicate justice? If the divinity of the emperor is just a constitutional fiction, why resist it? Is such behavior not dangerous illusion? Why not work out a compromise with the imperial powers and cults of Asia Minor and Rome? True, Jesus was executed by the Romans as a political criminal, but this was a theological misunderstanding of his claim to messiahship. Did not Paul, the great apostle, preach that Christians ought not to resist civil authorities but to give honor to whom honor is due (Rm 13)? To behave otherwise is religious fanaticism and foolishness.

It seems that some very established Christians in the churches of Asia Minor argued in such a theological vein. Since John polemizes against such Christians, whom he calls by Old Testament nicknames—Balaamites or followers of Jezebel or Nicolaitans—it is difficult to distill their genuine teachings from John's biting polemics. It is interesting that one of their renowned prophets was a woman who could claim the official title "prophet" while John never applies this title to himself, probably because his prophetic office was not officially acknowledged by all the churches. However, John does not argue against this woman prophet because she was a woman claiming prophetic office and leadership but because of her teachings.

This alternative Christian prophetic group seems to have approved of the Christian's participation in pagan cultic meals and in the imperial cult, a praxis which John consistently labels as "fornication." The expressions "eating meat sacrificed to idols" and to "know the deep things of Satan" give some clues about their theological argument and its legitimization. Like the Corinthians and Paul, they probably argued that "idols are nothing" and that "an idol has no real power" over those whom Christ has redeemed from the cosmic powers of this world. Therefore, participation in the everyday life of Greco-Roman society and in the formalities of the imperial cult is perfectly harmless for a spirit-filled Christian. God's and Christ's powers are of a completely different order than the political-religious order of Rome (cf. for such an argument Jn 18:36 ff). Like the author of the first Epistle of Peter, who also wrote to Christians in Asia Minor toward the end of the first century, they might have insisted: Be subject for the Lord's sake to every human institution, whether it be the emperor as supreme or the governors. . . . Fear God. Honor the emperor (1 P 2:13 f,17).

It is argued that the theology of the Nicolaitans was already gnostic and therefore heretic. We have very little evidence for such a categorization, but we do know that some New Testament writers advocated an acceptance of the Roman power structure. It seems that the difference in theological perspective is not so much doctrinal as it is rooted in a quite different experience of Roman power and influence in Asia Minor. Although we do not know the social situation of the prophetic Christian group against whom John competes, we do know that he himself and some of the communities to whom he writes have experienced poverty, banishment, violence, and assassination. Therefore, he views Roman power as exploitative, destructive, and dehumanizing. He, moreover, has only praise for the communities that are poor and have experienced harassment from their Jewish compatriots, but he has harsh criticism for the community of Laodicea that considers itself rich and prosperous. Therefore, the theology and mythological symbolization can only be perceived when their rootedness in the "jailhouse" experience of the author is understood.

Martin Luther King's "Letter from a Birmingham Jail" reflects experiences and hopes similar to those that determine the theology of Revelation. In the crude outline of this letter scribbled on toilet paper in jail, the following three topics emerge: First, the ethics of Christian commitment; second, the judgment of God upon the dehumanizing power of White America; and third, a glimpse of the New Jerusalem, echoing King's famous "I have a dream." Admittedly Martin Luther King was influenced by the theology of Revelation. Nevertheless, it was his experience of the oppression of his people and his own imprisonment that led him to underscore the political implications of Christian theology.

Revelation gives great prominence to the ethics of Christian commitment. This ethical-political interest prohibits Christians from projecting "evil" only on others, while holding themselves exempt from it. Revelation speaks not only of judgment against the dehumanizing antidivine powers but also warns Christians not to succumb to their very concrete pressures. The book therefore begins with a section of censure and exhortation to faithfulness. The major part of the work describes in mythological-symbolic language the threat of the Roman political and religious powers. They bring destruction not only to the Christians but to the whole world. Revelation highlights in mythological symbolization that God, the creator, and Christ, the liberator, are the true eschatological regents of this world. Therefore, the eternal gospel calls all the earth dwellers to repentance and the Christians to loyal resistance. Finally, the last section shows the glory, life, light, and happiness of God's salvation and empire, which is free from all oppressive powers and dehumanizing forces. The injunctions, beatitudes, warnings, and promises, which run through the book like a red string, have the function of motivating the audience, while the symbolic universe of vision gives meaning to their present experience of oppression and persecution. Yet it is important to keep in mind that Revelation's political-mythological language does not spiritualize human exploitation, oppression, and persecution but fully unmasks it as against God's intention. The outcry of Revelation for justice and judgment can only be fully understood by those who hunger and thirst for justice.

Revelation's vision of eschatological salvation and well-being and its denunciation of all destructive powers throughout Christian history have mostly inspired chiliastic movements rather than establishment Christianity. Whereas main-line Christianity often co-opted or neutralized Revelation's political-religious

language and vision by identifying God's empire with
the institutional church or with the interior salvation
of the soul, messianic-prophetic Christian movements
have again and again affirmed Revelation's vision of
salvation as total humanization and wholeness, and as
liberation from oppressive ecclesiastical structures and
from the destructive domination of those who have
power in this world. They have maintained that the
empire of God means salvation for this world and not
merely salvation from this world or salvation of the
soul. Oppressive political-societal-religious powers and
the life-giving empire and power of God cannot
coexist. Therefore, John's attempt to formulate the reality and meaning of eschatological salvation in universal and political symbols gains greater significance
again, at a time when those who share the author's experience of oppression and exploitation attempt to formulate their own theology of liberation and to stake
their life on it. It might very well be possible that we
will feel as helpless or resentful vis-à-vis such liberation theologies as we feel vis-à-vis the theology of Revelation. We will not be able to perceive their vision unless we also share the theological analysis of those who
experience our culture and society or our church as destructive.

A. *Prologue and Epistolary Greeting*
Revelation 1:1 to 1:8

INTRODUCTION

In order to understand Revelation it is important to pay attention to its structural composition. As do the prophetic books of the Old Testament so does Revelation begin with an elaborate introduction which has three parts: Similar to Amos 1:1-2, Revelation is prefaced with a title (1:1-3) and a motto (1:7-8). They announce both the content and the perspective of the book. The epistolary greeting inserted into the traditional form of the prophetic prologue is similar to that of the Pauline letters (1:4-6). This well-composed introduction thus formally characterizes Revelation as a work of prophecy that functions like an open pastoral letter addressed to seven Christian churches in Asia Minor (modern-day Turkey). The careful composition of the prologue as well as the injunctions to write (1:11,19) indicate that the author understands his work as a literary prophecy.

Revelation 1:1–3
THE TITLE

¹ **1** This is the revelation given by God to Jesus Christ so that he could tell his servants about the things which are now to take place very soon; he sent his angel to make it known to his servant ² John, ·and John has written down everything he saw and swears it is the word of God guaranteed ³ by Jesus Christ. ·Happy the man who reads this prophecy, and happy those who listen to him, if they treasure all that it says, because the Time is close.

✠

The title of Revelation describes in a very concise form its contents as well as the authority behind its chain of communication. The headline identifies the book as a "revelation (Gk: *apokalypsis*) of Jesus Christ" and as the "words of prophecy." The Greek word for revelation is found only here where it seems to function as a title for the whole work. It is, however, significant that the original title of the book is not "revelation" or "apocalypse" of John but of Jesus Christ. The popular title "Revelation of John" was only added when the book was accepted into the canon. It seems to be derived from the first three verses and was probably formulated in analogy to the titles of other Jewish and Christian apocalypses that were attributed to a great figure of the past, e.g., Abraham, Ezra, Baruch, or Peter.

As distinct from other Jewish and Christian apocalypses, Revelation does not claim the authority of John but that of Jesus Christ. In a similar fashion, Paul claims that he did not receive the Gospel from human authorities but he has learned it "only through a revelation of Jesus Christ" (Ga 1:12 ff). Since the full name "Jesus Christ" occurs only in the title (1:1,2) and in the epistolary greeting (1:5), the author appears to be deliberately referring to the Pauline linguistic and theological understanding of "apocalypse" which is almost synonymous with the gift of prophecy (cf. 1 Co 14). Therefore, he can alternate the book's characterization as "revelation of Jesus Christ" with the expression "the words of prophecy."

The "words of prophecy" have originated with God who gave them to Jesus Christ who in turn showed them, through an angel, to the Christian prophets and especially to the prophet John. They are words of encouragement that promise the imminent eschatological judgment and salvation: "The last time is at hand." What, according to God's plan, has to take place in the immediate future is revealed to the prophets. Although the expression "servants" can characterize all Christians, it probably designates here the Christian prophets. According to Amos 3:7, God does nothing without revealing it to the servants of God, the prophets. Now God reveals through Jesus Christ the final times to the Christian prophets.

That this revelation is said to be communicated through an angel corresponds to apocalyptic style. Moreover, that the prophecy is not told but "signified" or "shown" likewise indicates apocalyptic style. This literary apocalyptic style is similar to that of poetry insofar as it does not explain and logically argue but expresses its vision in literary symbols and images. This first section of the prologue is concluded with a macarism or blessing. It indicates that Revelation is conceived as a literary work intended to be read in the assembly of the community. Anyone who has ever "listened" to the whole book will agree that it comes much more alive when read aloud to an audience. We know from the Pauline letters and the Didachē that, ordinarily, Christian prophets would have spoken in the liturgical congregation. During his absence, John intends his work to function as such a prophetic utterance in the worship of the churches.

Revelation 1:4–6
EPISTOLARY GREETING

4 From John, to the seven churches of Asia: grace and peace to you from him who is, who was, and who is to come, from the seven spirits 5 in his presence before his throne, ·and from Jesus Christ, the faithful witness, the First-born from the dead, the Ruler of the kings of the earth. He loves us and has washed away our sins with his 6 blood, ·and made us a line of kings, priests to serve his God and Father; to him, then, be glory and power for ever and ever. Amen.

✠

To assure the acceptance of the prophecy in the churches, John sends his work in the form of the by then already traditional Pauline epistle. As do the opening greetings of the Pauline letters, the epistolary introduction here also mentions the sender, John, and the recipients, the seven churches. Unlike other apocalypses, Revelation is not pseudonymous and does not derive its authority from a person of the past, but mentions its writer by name. Although ecclesiastical tradition has identified the author of Revelation with the apostle John, such an identification is not very likely, since Revelation 21:14 speaks of the twelve apostles as figures of the past. We therefore are no longer able to say who the prophet John actually was. Yet he must have been known and respected by the churches to which he writes, since he does not need any further introduction or authorization.

John, like Paul, replaces the standard Hellenistic greeting with the expression "grace and peace." However, John greatly expands Paul's usual formula "from God, the Father, and the Lord Jesus Christ." Grace and peace come from God, who is characterized in a threefold way, from the seven spirits, and from Jesus Christ, to whom the concluding doxology ascribes glory and power forever. Three titles rooted in early Christian tradition characterize Jesus Christ in relationship to the Christian community: He is the eschatological witness on whom the Christians can rely; he is the inaugurator and representative of the new creation; and, finally, he is the ruler who has all kingship and power. The three titles of Christ are paralleled by three statements about the activity of Christ that are rooted in the early Christian baptismal tradition. Christ loves us, the baptized, whom he has freed through his death from our personal sins, and whom he has installed as priestly members of the kingdom or empire created for God, the Father.

Revelation 1:7–8
THE MOTTO

⁷ It is he who is coming on the clouds; everyone
will see him, even those who pierced him, and all
the races of the earth will mourn over him. This
⁸ is the truth. Amen. •"I am the Alpha and the
Omega" says the Lord God, who is, who was,
and who is to come, the Almighty.

✠

The conclusion of the prologue consists of a prophetic
announcement of Christ's Parousia (coming) (1:7)
that is followed by an explicit word of God (1:8).

The prophetic announcement of the Parousia indicates how deeply the author is steeped in Old Testament and early Christian traditions. He does not quote
them but uses the tradition as a language arsenal for
his own prophetic statements. Revelation 1:7 seems to
be a textual conflation of Daniel 7:13 and Zechariah
12:10. It shares its eschatological tenor with the announcement of the Parousia in Matthew 24:30, but it
does not mention the Synoptic title "Son of Man" (or
Human Offspring), probably because this Christological title was not too familiar to the post-Pauline
churches. Revelation also shares its allusion to Zecha-

riah 12:10 (They shall look on the one whom they have pierced) with John 19:37b. At his Parousia, Christ will appear on the clouds of heaven and his sovereignty will be openly manifested to the whole world. This return of Christ will mean judgment and calamity to those who have killed him (cf. 19:11 ff).

The prophetic announcement of the glorious vindication of Christ before the whole world concludes with a vigorous confirmation that combines Greek and Hebrew (This is the truth, Amen). It is God who guarantees that this prophetic announcement will come to pass. Only here and in 21:5 does God speak directly. The first and last letter of the Greek alphabet characterize God as the "Beginning and the End." The designations, "who is, who was, and who is to come," refer back to 1:4 and climax in the title "the Almighty" or better "the ruler of the whole world." That this is the main title for God in Revelation (cf. 4:8; 11:7; 15:3; 16:7,14; 19:6,15; 21:22) indicates that the deepest theological concern for Revelation is the issue of power.

In conclusion: The introduction characterizes Revelation both in form and in content as an open prophetic letter. The apocalyptic visions, auditions, symbols, and images are set in an epistolary-prophetic framework. The theological focus of the introduction is Christological insofar as it speaks of Christ's revelation to the prophets, his redemptive activity in establishing and loving the community, and his eschatological public manifestation before the world. This "revelation of Jesus Christ" has, as its source and guarantee, God, the ruler of the universe.

STUDY QUESTION: What is your understanding of Revelation? Prepare a liturgy in which the whole book can be read aloud.

B. *The Prophetic Messages to the Churches*
Revelation 1:9 to 3:22

INTRODUCTION

This section allows us to study the careful composition of Revelation. After explicitly introducing the author and his situation, the prophetic inaugural vision expands into seven prophetic messages or proclamations. The compositional technique of inclusion ties this section to the whole of the book, whose major section begins (1:9) and concludes (22:8f) with an emphatic introduction and identification of the author: "I John." Moreover, the inaugural vision is framed by the command to write a visionary account and send it to the seven communities (1:11,19). Revelation thus is clearly intended to be a literary work, although it claims prophetic experience and inspiration.

The prophetic inaugural vision is well composed. It follows closely the outline and content of Daniel 10 but deviates from this copy in order to express its own theological emphasis. Like the vision in Daniel, the inaugural vision 1:12–19 has two parts: a vision (I saw . . . cf. 1:12) and an audition (He said . . . cf. 1:17). However, the author alters the text of Daniel 10 with features from Daniel 7 (someone like a human figure and the description of the hair), from Exodus (robe and girdle) and from Ezekiel (feet and voice). Moreover, he expands the audition with an "I am saying" derived from early Christian tradition. (I am the first and last. . . .) Finally he adds an allegorical interpretation in 1:20.

The so-called seven letters are not real letters but formalized prophetic proclamations to the churches. They are carefully structured and each message follows a definite pattern which consists of the following elements:

1. The command to write
2. The prophetic-messenger formula and the characterization of the speaker, Jesus Christ
3. The "I know" section whose elements and sequence can vary:

   a. description of situation (I know that . . .)
   b. censure (But I have against you . . .)
   c. command to repent
   d. a prophetic-revelatory saying (look . . .)
   e. promise of the Lord's speedy coming
   f. exhortation (hold fast)

4. The call to hear addressed to everyone in the churches
5. The eschatological promise to those who will overcome.

The characterizations of Jesus Christ repeat features of the inaugural vision and in this way stress that the messages are a part of this vision. Moreover, the characterizations of Jesus Christ, and especially the eschatological promises, are all again taken up in the final section of the book. The first and last section thus stand in close relationship with each other and frame the central section of the book. Finally, despite their structural uniformity, the seven messages are not repetitive or monotonous. Four of them contain praise and censure, two communities receive only praise and one, only censure.

That the author writes in his own name distinguishes him from other apocalyptic writers who often claimed a great figure of the past (e.g., Moses, Enoch, Baruch) as the author of their work in order to gain a fictive standpoint in the past from where they could present past history in the form of pronouncement for the future. John does not employ such a pseudonym because he is not interested in communicating esoteric knowledge and prediction but in providing prophetic interpretation and eschatological exhortation for the Christian community of Asia Minor. The so-called seven letters therefore have structurally the same position that surveys of world history, reviews of heavenly secrets, or the description of heavenly journeys hold in other apocalypses. They therefore must not be separated from the following so-called apocalyptic visions but must be understood as an integral part of the overall composition.

Revelation 1:9
THE SOLIDARITY OF JOHN
WITH HIS READERS

9 My name is John, and through our union in Jesus I am your brother and share your sufferings, your kingdom, and all you endure. I was on the island of Patmos for having preached God's word and witnessed for Jesus;

✠

Revelation 1:9–11 does not only provide the setting for the introductory call vision of the prophet John but also characterizes the historical-theological setting of the whole book. Like the Hebrew prophets, John identifies his own standpoint in his own day and age. His "words of prophecy" seek to strengthen the congregation in Asia Minor in their severe clash with the antidivine and dehumanizing powers of their society. Like the early Christian prophets, he exercises his prophetic leadership for the "upbuilding, encouragement, and consolation" (1 Co 14:3) of the community. He derives the authority to do so not only from his prophetic inspiration but also from the solidarity and common experience that he shares with the Christians to whom he writes. Therefore, he does not introduce himself with the title prophet or teacher but as their "brother and partner."

The three Greek expressions that characterize the theological and historical situation of John and his readers are very difficult to translate. The first word *thlipsis* can be translated as "agony, distress, ordeal, eschatological tribulation, suffering, or oppression." John thus shares with the Christians of Asia Minor the tribulations of the endtime such as exile and imprisonment, social ostracism, slander, poverty, economic exploitation, violence, and the constant threat of judicial action and execution of which the book speaks. Although it is debated whether John was on the island of Patmos because of prophetic inspiration or because he was penalized with exile, the latter is more likely. Because of his prophetic activity and his preaching of Christ, John has already experienced the persecution and harassment which threaten the Christian churches in Asia Minor.

The second term—*basileia*—again can be translated into English in different ways as "kingdom, empire, royal power, kingship, sovereignty, or dominion." John and the communities participate in the eschatological power of God's and Christ's kingly reign and are partners in God's empire now. The Christians are appointed in baptism as members of God's kingdom or empire, and they will exercise their royal power in the eschatological future. Therefore, the power of Satan represented by the Roman empire must lead to violent actions against the Christians whose loyalty belongs to the kingdom and empire of God. In Revelation, power is set against power and empire against empire. Compromise is not possible.

Therefore, the main Christian "virtue" in Revelation is not faith or love but *hypomone* which can mean

"patience, loyal endurance, consistent resistance, steadfastness, perseverance, or staying power." The junc-
ture of the oppression of the eschatological tribulations with the claim of partnership in the divine empire
and kingly power demands consistent resistance and
steadfast perseverance. This is the task of the Christians who are the representatives of God's power and
kingdom here and now.

STUDY QUESTION: What do you know about early
Christian prophecy? What is John's
understanding of the ministry?

of the seven golden lampstands. If then the seven
stars are... figures of the seven churches, and
the seven lampstands are the seven churches
also...

Revelation 1:10–20
THE LORD AND JUDGE
OF THE CHURCH

10 it was the Lord's day and the Spirit possessed me,
and I heard a voice behind me, shouting like a
11 trumpet, ·"Write down all that you see in a book,
and send it to the seven churches of Ephesus,
Smyrna, Pergamum, Thyatira, Sardis, Philadel-
12 phia and Laodicea." ·I turned around to see who
had spoken to me, and when I turned I saw seven
13 golden lampstands ·and, surrounded by them, a
figure like a Son of man, dressed in a long robe
14 tied at the waist with a golden girdle. ·His head
and his hair were white as white wool or as snow,
15 his eyes like a burning flame, ·his feet like burnished bronze when it has been refined in a furnace, and his voice like the sound of the ocean.
16 In his right hand he was holding seven stars, out
of his mouth came a sharp sword, double-edged,
and his face was like the sun shining with all its
force.
17   When I saw him, I fell in a dead faint at his
feet, but he touched me with his right hand and
said, "Do not be afraid; it is I, the First and the
18 Last; I am the Living One, ·I was dead and now
I am to live for ever and ever, and I hold the
19 keys of death and of the underworld. ·Now write
down all that you see of present happenings and
20 things that are still to come. ·The secret of the
seven stars you have seen in my right hand, and

of the seven golden lampstands is this: the seven
stars are the angels of the seven churches, and
the seven lampstands are the seven churches
themselves.

✠

Like the Old Testament prophets, John introduces
his message with a prophetic call vision. He mentions
the place (Patmos) and time (probably Sunday) when
the vision took place. However, John does not claim
that he received his prophetic vocation in ecstasy, but
simply uses the classic prophetic formula "The Spirit
came upon me." He also does not say that he wrote the
whole book during or immediately after the vision as
popular understanding has it.

A careful look at the inaugural vision can demonstrate why it is justified to call Revelation a "literary
vision." It is impossible to picture or draw this vision.
Revelation is full of images which cannot be imaged.
The images and symbols function more like words and
sentences in a composition. One could say that the author constructs his paragraph and section with symbols
and images rather than with abstract concepts and
theological definitions.

A comparison of the figure in Daniel 10 with that of
Christ in Revelation 1 indicates that John works in a
literary fashion insofar as he closely follows Daniel
10 but differs from it in several instances. These
differences point to the aspects which the author
wanted to stress or to add. Whereas Daniel 10:5 refers
to a human person, Revelation refers here and in
14:14 to someone like a human offspring, probably in
order to allude to the early Christian "Son of Man"

title without explicitly mentioning it. The description of
the hair (cf. Dn 7) and of the voice (cf. Ez 1:14;
43:2) underlines the affinity of Christ to God. Moreover, while the human figure in Daniel 10 is clothed in
linen and wears the girdle around the hips, the Christ
figure in Revelation is clothed like the Jewish high
priest in a long robe (cf. Ez 9:2; Ex 28:4,31) and
girded around the breast (cf. Ez 44:18). These explicit changes of the Daniel text seem to stress Christ's
royal/priestly character, since in New Testament times
the high priest had not just cultic but also kingly functions and honors. The two-edged sword, finally,
identifies Christ as the judge of the communities (cf.
also Rv 2:16), whereas this symbol designates him in
19:15 as judge of the nations. Thus the first and last
sections of Revelation open with the image of Christ as
the eschatological judge. However, Revelation does not
just threaten judgment to the nations but also places
the community under the judgment of Christ. In doing
so John seeks to prevent Christians from projecting evil
and failure only onto others without acknowledging
that they themselves are accountable for their own actions. At the same time he assures them that Christ not
only has conquered death but that he, as the Living
One, has control also over the destructive powers of
death.

The inaugural vision's main interests therefore focus
on the present relationship of Christ to the Christian
community. John underlines this in 1:20 by explicitly
interpreting two features of the inaugural vision that
picture Christ as standing in the midst of seven golden
lampstands, holding seven stars in his right hand. The
seven candelabra have the same form as the golden
temple menorah which in New Testament times was a
symbol of the Jewish people. Revelation 1:20 identifies

them with the Christian communities to whom Revelation is addressed. The images of 1:12 f and 2:1 seem thus to express the same theological notion as Leviticus 26:12: "I will walk among you and will be your God and you shall be my people." The Christological reality is here only symbolically signified but it will be open reality in the eschatological future, when God will live among the people of God (21:3).

The image of the seven stars in the right hand of Christ is more difficult to understand since we do not find it in the Old Testament. The seven stars seem to refer to the seven planets that were a symbol of the universal dominion of the Roman emperors. This symbol, then, characterizes Christ in analogy to the Roman emperor as universal ruler of the world. However, the interpretation which is given in 1:20 does not quite correspond to this interpretation since the seven stars are identified with the angels of the churches to whom the prophetic messages are addressed. Since Revelation does not mention bishops anywhere else, it is unlikely that bishops are addressed here. Because angels in Revelation are usually heavenly beings, it is more likely that the seven angels are the patron angels of the churches. Since the angel and the prophet are very closely related (cf. 19:10; 22:9), it is possible that the angels represent the prophetic spirit and prophetic leadership in the communities. This interpretation is supported not only by the fact that John seems to be the head of a prophetic school or circle (22:9) but also by the fact that in the conclusion of the individual messages it is the spirit who speaks to the communities. The interpretation of the seven stars in 1:20 would then focus Christ's universal power on his relationship to the Christian churches. He exercises his authority over them through the prophetic word and the eschatological promises of the spirit.

STUDY QUESTIONS: How does this image of Jesus Christ relate to your personal image of Christ? Can you relate to this image?

Revelation 2:1–3:22
PROPHETIC CENSURE
AND ENCOURAGEMENT

The so-called seven letters are a formal part of the inaugural vision and follow a definite compositional pattern. Therefore, they should not be understood as real
letters that were later incorporated into the book but as
prophetic messages, symbolized by the number seven,
addressing the whole church in Asia Minor. Geographically all communities are situated on a main
Roman road and form a circuit starting from Ephesus,
the nearest city to Patmos. They represent the church
in Asia Minor that was one of the main centers of early
Christianity. Since the messages are not just addressed
to individual communities but were designed to be read
by all of them, it seems justified not to discuss them sep-
arately but to attempt a cumulative analysis of the overall situation. The so-called seven letters are not private
messages. Instead, they have the literary function of focusing the book as a whole on the situation of the entire
church in this region. Thus the seven messages give a
realistic but stylized picture of the church in Asia Minor
insofar as John points to the strengths and weaknesses
of these churches.

The main objective of this section is prophetic exhortation and critical evaluation. The strong aspects of

the church in Asia Minor are mutual love, service for others, fidelity and steadfastness, the keeping of the Lord's word and the rejection of the false teachers, confession of their faith in persecutions and consistent resistance. The author stresses very much the "works" or the praxis of the Asian church. Yet not all the churches are still doing "the works of their first love." Some do not reject the false teachers, some are no longer "alive," and some of them are "tepid" and in danger of being cast away. The main call is therefore the call to "remember" what Christ did for them, to repent and radically change their orientation and commitment, and to endure and hold on to what they have.

1. Ephesus

1 2 "Write to the angel of the church in Ephesus and say, 'Here is the message of the one who holds the seven stars in his right hand and who lives surrounded by the seven golden lamp-
2 stands: ·I know all about you: how hard you work and how much you put up with. I know you cannot stand wicked men, and how you tested the impostors who called themselves apostles and
3 proved they were liars. ·I know, too, that you have patience, and have suffered for my name
4 without growing tired. ·Nevertheless, I have this complaint to make; you have less love now than
5 you used to. ·Think where you were before you fell; repent, and do as you used to at first, or else, if you will not repent, I shall come to you and
6 take your lamp-stand from its place. ·It is in your favor, nevertheless, that you loathe as I do what
7 the Nicolaitans are doing. ·If anyone has ears to hear, let him listen to what the Spirit is saying to the churches: those who prove victorious I will feed from the tree of life set in God's paradise.'

2. Smyrna

8 "Write to the angel of the church in Smyrna and say, 'Here is the message of the First and the Last, who was dead and has come to life again:
9 I know the trials you have had, and how poor you are—though you are rich—and the slanderous accusations that have been made by the people who profess to be Jews but are really members of
10 the synagogue of Satan. ·Do not be afraid of the sufferings that are coming to you: I tell you, the devil is going to send some of you to prison to test you, and you must face an ordeal for ten days. Even if you have to die, keep faithful, and I will
11 give you the crown of life for your prize. ·If anyone has ears to hear, let him listen to what the Spirit is saying to the churches: for those who prove victorious there is nothing to be afraid of in the second death.'

3. Pergamum

12 "Write to the angel of the church in Pergamum and say, 'Here is the message of the one who has
13 the sharp sword, double-edged: ·I know where you live, in the place where Satan is enthroned, and that you still hold firmly to my name, and did not disown your faith in me even when my faithful witness, Antipas, was killed in your own town, where Satan lives.
14 Nevertheless, I have one or two complaints to make: some of you are followers of Balaam, who taught Balak to set a trap for the Israelites so that they committed adultery by eating food that had
15 been sacrificed to idols; ·and among you, too, there are some as bad who accept what the Nico-
16 laitans teach. ·You must repent, or I shall soon come to you and attack these people with the
17 sword out of my mouth. ·If anyone has ears to hear, let him listen to what the Spirit is saying to the churches: to those who prove victorious I will give the hidden manna and a white stone—a stone with a new name written on it, known only to the man who receives it.'

4. Thyatira

18 "Write to the angel of the church in Thyatira and say, 'Here is the message of the Son of God who has eyes like a burning flame and feet like
19 burnished bronze: ·I know all about you and how charitable you are; I know your faith and devotion and how much you put up with, and I know
20 how you are still making progress. ·Nevertheless, I have a complaint to make: you are encouraging the woman Jezebel who claims to be a prophetess, and by her teaching she is luring my servants away to commit the adultery of eating food which
21 has been sacrificed to idols. ·I have given her time to reform but she is not willing to change her
22 adulterous life. ·Now I am consigning her to bed, and all her partners in adultery to troubles that will test them severely, unless they repent of their
23 practices; ·and I will see that her children die, so that all the churches realize that it is I who search heart and loins and give each one of you what
24 your behavior deserves. ·But on the rest of you in Thyatira, all of you who have not accepted this teaching or learned the secrets of Satan, as they
25 are called, I am not laying any special duty; ·but hold firmly on to what you already have until I
26 come. ·To those who prove victorious, and keep
27 working for me until the end, I will give the ·au-
28 thority over the pagans ·which I myself have been given by my Father, to rule them with an iron sceptre and shatter them like earthenware. And
29 I will give him the Morning Star. ·If anyone has ears to hear, let him listen to what the Spirit is saying to the churches.'

5. Sardis

1 3 "Write to the angel of the church in Sardis and say, 'Here is the message of the one who holds the seven spirits of God and the seven stars: I know all about you: how you are reputed to be
2 alive and yet are dead. ·Wake up; revive what little you have left: it is dying fast. So far I have failed to notice anything in the way you live that

³ my God could possibly call perfect, ·and yet do
you remember how eager you were when you first
heard the message? Hold on to that. Repent. If
you do not wake up, I shall come to you like a
thief, without telling you at what hour to expect
⁴ me. ·There are a few in Sardis, it is true, who have
kept their robes from being dirtied, and they are
⁵ fit to come with me, dressed in white. ·Those who
prove victorious will be dressed, like these, in
white robes; I shall not blot their names out of the
book of life, but acknowledge their names in the
⁶ presence of my Father and his angels. ·If anyone
has ears to hear, let him listen to what the Spirit
is saying to the churches.'

6. Philadelphia

⁷ "Write to the angel of the church in Philadelphia and say, 'Here is the message of the holy and
faithful one who has the key of David, so that
when he opens, nobody can close, and when he
⁸ closes, nobody can open: ·I know all about you;
and now I have opened in front of you a door
that nobody will be able to close—and I know that
though you are not very strong, you have kept my
commandments and not disowned my name.
⁹ Now I am going to make the synagogue of Satan
—those who profess to be Jews, but are liars, because they are no such thing—I will make them
come and fall at your feet and admit that you are
¹⁰ the people that I love. ·Because you have kept
my commandment to endure trials, I will keep
you safe in the time of trial which is going to
come for the whole world, to test the people of
¹¹ the world. ·Soon I shall be with you: hold firmly
to what you already have, and let nobody take
¹² your prize away from you. ·Those who prove victorious I will make into pillars in the sanctuary of
my God, and they will stay there for ever; I will
inscribe on them the name of my God and the
name of the city of my God, the new Jerusalem
which comes down from my God in heaven, and

¹³ my own new name as well. ·If anyone has ears to hear, let him listen to what the Spirit is saying to the churches.'

7. Laodicea

¹⁴   "Write to the angel of the church in Laodicea and say, 'Here is the message of the Amen, the faithful, the true witness, the ultimate source of ¹⁵ God's creation: ·I know all about you: how you are neither cold nor hot. I wish you were one or ¹⁶ the other, ·but since you are neither, but only ¹⁷ lukewarm, I will spit you out of my mouth. ·You say to yourself, "I am rich, I have made a fortune, and have everything I want," never realizing that you are wretchedly and pitiably poor, and blind ¹⁸ and naked too. ·I warn you, buy from me the gold that has been tested in the fire to make you really rich, and white robes to clothe you and cover your shameful nakedness, and eye ointment to put on ¹⁹ your eyes so that you are able to see. ·I am the one who reproves and disciplines all those he loves: ²⁰ so repent in real earnest. ·Look, I am standing at the door, knocking. If one of you hears me calling and opens the door, I will come in to share his ²¹ meal, side by side with him. ·Those who prove victorious I will allow to share my throne, just as I was victorious myself and took my place with ²² my Father on his throne. ·If anyone has ears to hear, let him listen to what the Spirit is saying to the churches.' "

✠

What was the concrete political situation and theological issue in the seven churches? Revelation indicates that they have already experienced discriminations and persecutions from the Jewish population as well as from the Roman provincial authorities. Their precarious societal and religious situations were fostered by two major developments which had occurred under the Flavian emperors Vespasian (69–79), Titus (79–81), and Domitian (81–96).

First: Under the Flavians, especially Domitian, the imperial cult was strongly promoted in the Roman provinces. Domitian demanded that the populace acclaim him as "Lord and God" and participate in his worship. Such a participation in the emperor cult and state religion was regarded as a sign of political loyalty since the emperor was the living head of the state and the guardian of its fortunes.

The majority of the cities to which the prophetic messages are addressed were dedicated to the promotion of the Roman civil religion. Ephesus, the greatest city of the Roman province Asia, was the seat of the proconsul and competed with Pergamum for the recognition of its primacy. Like Smyrna it was a center of the emperor cult and famous for its gladiatorial games. Pergamum, a citadel of Hellenic civilization in Asia, was the official center of the imperial cult. Already, in 29 B.C., the city had received permission to build a temple to the "divine Augustus and the goddess Roma" which is identified in Revelation as the "throne of Satan." In Thyatira the emperor was worshiped as Apollo incarnate and as the son of Zeus. In A.D. 26, Sardis competed with ten other Asian cities for the right of building a temple in honor of the emperor but lost out to Smyrna. Laodicea was not only the wealthiest city of Phrygia but also a center of the imperial cult. In such an environment the Christians were bound to experience increasing conflicts with the Roman civil religion since they acclaimed Jesus Christ and not the emperor as their "Lord and God." It is true that we do not know of a full-fledged, legally sanctioned persecution of Christians before the second century, but the author of Revelation has experienced political exile and knows of persecutions of individual Christians (cf. Antipas). He anticipates an increase of persecutions and sufferings for the near future, not least because of the increasing totalitarianism of the reign of Domitian.

Second: This situation was aggravated because Jewish Christians like John could less and less claim the Jewish political privileges for themselves. The Jews had the privilege of practicing their religion in any part of the empire and were exempted from military service and the imperial cult. However, under the Flavians their situation had become more precarious. Vespasian ordered that all Jews and proselytes now had to pay a special tax to the Romans in place of the tax formerly paid to the Jerusalem temple. Domitian enforced the tax and singled out for payment especially the proselytes and God-fearers who were not Jews by birth. Since, after the destruction of Jerusalem and the temple, the Jewish community was forced to define more and more its religious boundaries and therefore to exclude Christians from the synagogue, such Jewish Christians no longer could claim the protection granted to the Jewish religion by Rome. The messages to Smyrna and Philadelphia reflect this conflict. John's identification of the synagogue as a congregation of Satan should not be misread as anti-Semitism since Revelation indicates great appreciation for true Judaism. But as a Jewish Christian, John is aware that the rich Jewish communities will not tolerate the deviance of the Christians who seemed to have been poor and powerless in Smyrna and Philadelphia. The Christians of Philadelphia, whose names were cast out from the synagogue and thus lost their share in the eschatological messianic future, are assured that Christ is the Davidic Messiah who will keep open the "door" to the eschatological empire and guarantee their citizenship in the New Jerusalem.

This everyday experience of harassment, persecution, and hostility from their Jewish as well as their pagan neighbors challenged the Christians' faith in Christ as the Lord and King of the world. The Christians experienced again and again that their situation in no way supported their theological conviction that they already participated in Christ's kingship and power. This tension between theological conviction and experienced reality must have provoked difficult theological problems: Why do the Christians have to suffer if Christ is the true Lord and King of the world? Why are the Christians persecuted if the living God is on their side and the gods of the other religions are powerless idols? Why did Christ not return in glory to prevent further suffering of the Christian communities? These pressing theological questions seem to have been answered differently by leading prophets in the church of Asia Minor. Revelation implicitly informs us of this theological argument by arguing against rival Christian apostles and prophets who had great influence within several of the communities.

Revelation explicitly polemizes against these rival Christian prophets in the messages to the churches in Ephesus, Pergamum, and Thyatira. Ephesus is praised for its rejection of the false apostles and its hatred for the works of the Nicolaitans, whereas Pergamum is criticized for tolerating those who hold the teachings of Balaam. The community in Thyatira, in turn, is censured for accepting the influence and teaching of a woman prophet and her school. It is probable that all three names "Nicolaitans, Balaam, and Jezebel" metaphorically characterize the same group of Christian prophets who allowed eating food sacrificed to idols and accepted religious syncretism. This theological stance had great political, economic, and professional advantages for the Christians living in the prosperous trading cities of Asia Minor, for the meat sacrificed to idols was served at meetings of trade guilds and business associations as well as private receptions. This alternative prophetic position thus proposed a theological compromise that allowed Christian citizens to participate actively in the commercial, political, and social life of their cities.

How did they argue theologically for such an integration into the pagan society? As the Hellenistic Jewish Christians in Corinth had done some forty years earlier, so they might have reasoned that "idols are nothing" (cf. 1 Co 8:4) and that therefore Christians could eat food previously sacrificed to them. Since the Christians, much more than any educated Roman or Asian, knew that Caesar's claim to divinity was nothing more than a constitutional fiction to promote political loyalty to Rome, why should they refuse to pay this honor to the emperor? Did not the great apostle Paul, who had founded some of the communities, demand that one submit to the authorities of the state because they were ordained by God (Rm 13:1–7)? That a Christian of Asia Minor at the end of the first century did argue in such a way is evident from 1 Peter who admonishes persecuted Christians: "Honor the emperor" (2:17). Since participation in the imperial cult did not demand creedal adherence, it was possible to honor the emperor without compromising one's faith in Jesus Christ.

Moreover, to oppose the imperial cult and to refuse

participation in societal-religious affairs would mean to take the sovereignty claims of the emperor and the reality of idols too seriously. The political claim of the emperor and state on the one hand and the religious claim of God and Christ on the other hand are not in conflict because both claims belong to a radically different order (cf. Jn 18:36–38). Jesus Christ's claim to kingship and power is not of a political nature but pertains to the Christian spiritual life and the religious dimension of the church, since the Christians are taken out of this world and by virtue of their baptism already share in the kingly power of their Lord. No one, not even Satan, can harm the elect Christians, for they have insights into the very depth of the demonic or divine. If this is the case, why go to prison for a cause which is not worth dying for? Is it not true that idols have no real existence and what else is the imperial image than an idol? To say otherwise would be bad theology or religious fanaticism.

In responding to this theological challenge John, like Paul before him, stresses that behind idols stands the demonic power of Satan, the ultimate adversary of God and the Christians. Therefore, no compromise is possible between loyalty to God and to Caesar because God and Christ are the true rulers of the world and the nations. This different theological response of John is rooted in a different social-political experience. He himself has experienced exile and persecution because of his witness to Jesus. Moreover, the two communities that deserve Christ's praise and receive no censure are obviously poor and without power. On the other hand the communities that receive only censure are rich, complacent, and do not experience any harassment either from the pagans or the Jews. It seems therefore that John advocates an uncompromising Christian theology because, for him and his followers, the dehumanizing powers of Rome and its vassals have become so destructive and oppressive that a compromise with them would mean a denial of God's life-giving, saving power. Therefore, the image of Christ in the inaugural vision stresses that he is alive, although he was killed. Those who will resist the powers of death determining their lives now will share in the power of Jesus Christ. To those who are poor and exploited, the "promises to the victor" guarantee the essentials of life for the eschatological future: food, clothing, home, citizenship, security, honor, power. These promises are made not to the rich, the satisfied, and the influential Christians but to those who are poor, persecuted, and suffering.

STUDY QUESTIONS: It is said that Revelation's theology is sub-Christian because it expresses the resentment of the "have-nots" but not the Christian spirit of the Sermon on the Mount. Do you think that such a judgment is justified? How is prophetic criticism of the church expressed today? What are the limitations of the political theology proposed by John?

C. Christ: The Eschatological Liberator and Regent
Revelation 4:1 to 9:21

INTRODUCTION

The opening remark links the visions of chapters 4–5
to the preceding seven series of the prophetic messages
by identifying the speaker (the first trumpet voice)
with that introducing the inaugural vision in 1:10,12
(a voice like a trumpet). Moreover, the last eschatological promise to the victors (3:21 f) does not only
point to the image of the throne as the central symbol
of the New Jerusalem but also to the following chapters 4–5 that envision the throne of God and show that
the victorious Christ has taken over his share in God's
ruling power. By taking possession of the sevenfold
sealed scroll, the Lamb is enthroned as the eschatological Lord of the world who executes the three
series of the plague septets in order to liberate the new
Exodus people of God. The opening of the seals en-
genders the seven cycles of the eschatological trumpets
(8:2–9:21; 11:15–19) whose plagues in turn are in-
tensified by the bowl septet (15:1,5–16:21). All three
plague septets refer to the same eschatological signs
and expound the traditional characteristics of the endtime. Therefore, the sequence of the plagues is not tem-
poral-chronological but thematic-schematical.

Revelation 4:1–5:14
GOD, THE CREATOR,
AND CHRIST, THE LIBERATOR

Although the seven seals belong integrally to chapters 4–5 and the four chapters should be read as a total unit, I have here separated them from the introductory vision for pragmatic reasons. This is justified methodologically since chapters 4–5 do not only provide the setting for the breaking of the seals but are also basic for the understanding of the whole work. Their central image, the throne (4:2,3,4,5,6,9,10; 5:1,6,7,11,13), is repeated again and again like a keynote throughout the whole book (1:4; 2:13; 3:21; 6:16; 7:9,10,11,15,17; 8:3; 11:16; 12:5; 13:2; 14:3; 16:10,17; 19:4,5; 20:4,11,12; 21:5; 22:1,3). Thus chapters 4–5 furnish the foundation and provide the assurance for all that follows. God enthroned in eternal majesty and power and the victorious Christ exercise true lordship over the world. Thus chapters 4–5 develop in the visionary language of symbol and myth the statement of Christ in 3:21 that he has conquered and therefore shares in the throne and power of God. The central theological question of these chapters as well as of the whole book is: Who is the true Lord of this world? This theological problem is elaborated and solved in the cosmological imagery and political language of chapters 4–5.

¹ **4** Then, in my vision, I saw a door open in heaven and heard the same voice speaking to me, the voice like a trumpet, saying, "Come up here: I will show you what is to come in the fu-
² ture." ·With that, the Spirit possessed me and I saw a throne standing in heaven, and the One who
³ was sitting on the throne, ·and the Person sitting there looked like a diamond and a ruby. There was a rainbow encircling the throne, and this
⁴ looked like an emerald. ·Round the throne in a circle were twenty-four thrones, and on them I saw twenty-four elders sitting, dressed in white
⁵ robes with golden crowns on their heads. ·Flashes of lightning were coming from the throne, and the sound of peals of thunder, and in front of the throne there were seven flaming lamps burning,
⁶ the seven Spirits of God. ·Between the throne and myself was a sea that seemed to be made of glass, like crystal. In the center, grouped round the throne itself, were four animals with many eyes,
⁷ in front and behind. ·The first animal was like a lion, the second like a bull, the third animal had a human face, and the fourth animal was like a
⁸ flying eagle. ·Each of the four animals had six wings and had eyes all the way round as well as inside; and day and night they never stopped singing:

> "Holy, Holy, Holy
> is the Lord God, the Almighty;
> he was, he is and he is to come."

⁹ Every time the animals glorified and honored and gave thanks to the One sitting on the throne, who
¹⁰ lives for ever and ever, ·the twenty-four elders prostrated themselves before him to worship the One who lives for ever and ever, and threw down
¹¹ their crowns in front of the throne, saying, ·"You are our Lord and our God, you are worthy of

glory and honor and power, because you made all
the universe and it was only by your will that
everything was made and exists."

1 5 I saw that in the right hand of the One sitting
on the throne there was a scroll that had writing on back and front and was sealed with seven
2 seals. ·Then I saw a powerful angel who called
with a loud voice, "Is there anyone worthy to
3 open the scroll and break the seals of it?" ·But
there was no one, in heaven or on the earth or
under the earth, who was able to open the scroll
4 and read it. ·I wept bitterly because there was no-
5 body fit to open the scroll and read it, ·but one of
the elders said to me, "There is no need to cry: the
Lion of the tribe of Judah, the Root of David, has
triumphed, and he will open the scroll and the
seven seals of it."

6   Then I saw, standing between the throne with
its four animals and the circle of the elders, a
Lamb that seemed to have been sacrificed; it had
seven horns, and it had seven eyes, which are the
seven Spirits God has sent out all over the world.
7 The Lamb came forward to take the scroll from
the right hand of the One sitting on the throne,
8 and when he took it, the four animals prostrated
themselves before him and with them the twenty-
four elders; each one of them was holding a harp
and had a golden bowl full of incense made of
9 the prayers of the saints. ·They sang a new hymn:

"You are worthy to take the scroll
and break the seals of it,
because you were sacrificed, and with your blood
you bought men for God
of every race, language, people and nation
10 and made them a line of kings and priests,
to serve our God and to rule the world."

11   In my vision, I heard the sound of an immense
number of angels gathered round the throne and
the animals and the elders; there were ten thousand times ten thousand of them and thousands
12 upon thousands, ·shouting, "The Lamb that was

sacrificed is worthy to be given power, riches, wisdom, strength, honor, glory and blessing."

13 Then I heard all the living things in creation— everything that lives in the air, and on the ground, and under the ground, and in the sea, crying, "To the One who is sitting on the throne and to the Lamb, be all praise, honor, glory and power, for

14 ever and ever." •And the four animals said, "Amen"; and the elders prostrated themselves to worship.

✠

While the first seven cycle of the prophetic messages interprets the situation of the Asian churches from the perspective of the resurrected Christ, chapters 4–5 describe the heavenly reality of divine power from the perspective of the seer who, in a prophetic revelation, has received a glimpse of the world of God. John's artistic competence can be detected in his ability to integrate different features of Isaiah 6:1 ff; Ezekiel 1: 26–28; Daniel 7:9; 1 Kings 22:19; Enoch 39 f and Slavonic Enoch 20–22 into an overall picture of great magnificence. Instead of explaining every feature of the vision, one should first of all seek to gain an overall impression of the whole composition.

Heaven is pictured here not so much as a temple but as an oriental sovereign's throne hall. God is seen as the Enthroned in the splendor of unapproachable light surrounded by the highest beings of the celestial court. The polished pavement of the royal hall stretches out before the throne like a sea of crystal-clear glass mirroring the Enthroned's resplendent majesty. Lightnings, thunders, and voices—the traditional signs of the theophany—proceed from the throne. Burning before the throne are seven lamps of fire which are interpreted as the symbol of the divine Spirit. As befits the "King of kings" God is attended both by twenty-four angelic vassals seated on thrones and wearing crowns of gold as well as by the four living creatures, the representation of all of creation. Although exegetes widely disagree about the identity of the twenty-four elders and the four living beings, it seems to be clear that the author understands them as the royal court, which gives homage and praise to the all-powerful ruler of the universe. Therefore, the whole vision climaxes in the hymnic acclamation of the Creator.

The central figure of the whole vision is clearly God enthroned in great splendor and surrounded by a court of angelic principalities and powers. However, no attempt is made to visualize God in human form. The glorious being of the Enthroned manifests itself in the brilliance of light reflected by the precious stones of opaque, diamondlike jasper, blood-red sardis, and the colorless emerald refracting a rainbow of prismatic colors, the sign of God's covenant with creation.

The thrice-holy and worthy acclamation in verses 8–11 serves to underline the glory and power of the almighty Creator whose eschatological Parousia is assured. According to the Roman writer Tacitus, the Parthian king Tiridates placed his diadem before the image of Nero in order to give homage to the Roman emperor. Here, too, the twenty-four angelic vassal/ kings cast their crowns before the Enthroned, acknowledging the Creator in the political language of the day. Domitian was acclaimed as "Lord *and* God" and the acclamation "worthy are you" greeted the triumphal entrance of the emperor. It is not the Roman emperor but God, the Creator and all-powerful regent of this world, who deserves unceasing honor and homage.

The vision of chapter 5 must be understood in the context of chapter 4. The whole account is a well-composed unit consisting of concentric segments. After the description of the sealed scroll (1) follows the question of the angel searching for the one worthy to open the seals (2). The importance of this quest is underlined in a threefold way: through the silence of the cosmos (3), the weeping of the seer (4), and the consolation by the elder (5) that points to the one who is worthy. After the appearance of the Lamb before the heavenly court is announced, the Lamb takes over the scroll from the outstretched hand of the Enthroned (6–7).

As the description of the scene gradually expands to its climax, so also the conclusion of the heavenly praise proceeds in four steps. The "new song" (9–10) corresponds to the consolation by the elder (5); the hymn of the angels (11–12) to the weeping of the seer (4), the praise of the world (13) seems to be the counterpart to the silence of the world (3) and finally the affirmative Amen of the four living creatures and the adoration of the elders (14) is the answer to the question of the angel (2). Like chapter 4, chapter 5 also climaxes in the hymnic homage of the heavenly court.

The central figure of the composition is the Lamb, an image which occurs twenty-eight times in Revelation and always signifies the resurrected Christ. Although it is not clear why the author uses this image for Christ, his usage of the word and the image is quite different from that of the Fourth Gospel. The image invokes the notion of the paschal lamb, the sacrificial lambs of the temple, or the astrological sign of the Aries.

The Lamb is characterized as the victor who had to suffer death. That the author does not think in pictorial images, but formulates his theology in the form of a lit-

erary vision, becomes obvious when he characterizes
the Lamb as "lion of the tribe of Judah" and the "root
of David." Both titles designate Christ as the fulfillment of all messianic hopes. The "seven horns"
and the "seven eyes," which are identified as the seven
spirits sent out into all the earth, symbolize the fullness
of power and omniscient control over the world.
Therefore, the Lamb alone in the whole universe is
worthy to receive and open the sevenfold sealed book
or scroll.

The enigma of the sevenfold sealed scroll has received many different interpretations. However, it
seems best to derive its meaning from its compositional
context. According to ancient oriental mythology, the
highest God possesses books or plates in which the destiny of the world is inscribed. In the ritual enthronement of the great king, these books are given to the
king as a sign that he now has power over the world.
By stressing that only the Lamb was worthy to receive
the sealed scroll and to open its seals, the author pictures the enthronement of Jesus Christ as ruler of the
world and its destiny. This interpretation of the whole
vision is confirmed by 5:12 where the object of the
"taking over" or "receiving" is not the sevenfold sealed
book but expressions of power and honor. By opening
the seals, Christ sets in motion the eschatological
events and exercises his power. The Christians therefore can recognize even in the eschatological plagues
coming over the nation the powerful dominion of their
Lord.

The "new song" in 5:9–10 stresses three reasons
why Christ was worthy to assume the eschatological
reign over the world.

First: The Lamb is worthy because it suffered a violent death. The verb "slain" probably alludes to the slaughtering of the paschal lamb, an image used early in the Christian tradition to interpret Christ's execution (cf. 1 Co 5:7; 1 P 1:18). This image evokes the memory of Israel's exodus and liberation that was considered in Judaism as a prototype for the final eschatological salvation.

Second: The Lamb's worthiness is rooted in his activity as God's purchasing agent, who has traveled throughout the world to purchase people from all nations. This metaphoric language has most probably as its point of reference the ransom of prisoners of war who were deported to the countries of the victors and could be ransomed by a purchasing agent of their home country. The image also alludes to the Exodus tradition. As the blood of the paschal lamb signified the liberation of Israel from the bondage of Egypt, so has the death of Christ made possible the liberation of Christians from their universal bondage.

Third: The final reason given for the Lamb's worthiness mentions the positive goal of Christ's redemptive activity. As, according to Roman law, the freed prisoners of war were brought back home and reintegrated into their own nation, so those who were ransomed for God were liberated to be a "kingdom and priests" who will exercise their royal power in the eschatological future on earth. Just as the Exodus led to the constitution of Israel as a special empire and nation for Yahweh (Ex 19:6), so has Christ created the community of the redeemed as the "nation" on earth that now acknowledges and witnesses to the power and reign of God and Christ. As the empire for God, they are the anti-empire to the Roman empire. However only those Christians who, like Christ, have been victorious will exercise eschatological royal power.

STUDY QUESTIONS: Does Revelation 4 describe a heavenly liturgy? How does it define the relationship between kingship/power and liturgy/worship? What does this imply for the relationship of politics and religion? Why does Revelation formulate the theology of redemption and salvation in political terms and economic metaphors?

Revelation 6:1–17
THE GREAT TRIBULATION
OF THE ENDTIME

Formally, the series of the seven seals can clearly be divided into a series of four, two, and one visions. The first four seals are parallels and follow the same narrative pattern: After a command from the four living creatures follows the release of a rider and a horse. The conclusion stresses the destructive powers of the rider. The color of the horse is related to the function of the rider which in turn is symbolically elaborated by the attribute characterizing each rider. In comparison with the first four seals, the fifth and sixth seals are structured differently and are more elaborate. This indicates their significance for the overall structure. The twofold interlude preceding the opening of the last seal is very short and enigmatic. Formally, the opening of the seals gradually prepares us for the revelation of the scroll's content, yet the scroll is only opened when all seven seals are removed. The whole series shows many allusions to Old Testament texts but does not follow a certain pattern known from the Old Testament or other texts familiar to us. The whole literary vision is the work of the author.

¹ 6 Then I saw the Lamb break one of the seven seals, and I heard one of the four animals ² shout in a voice like thunder, "Come." ·Immediately a white horse appeared, and the rider on it was holding a bow; he was given the victor's crown and he went away, to go from victory to victory.

³ When he broke the second seal, I heard the ⁴ second animal shout, "Come." ·And out came another horse, bright red, and its rider was given this duty: to take away peace from the earth and set people killing each other. He was given a huge sword.

⁵ When he broke the third seal, I heard the third animal shout, "Come." Immediately a black horse appeared, and its rider was holding a pair of ⁶ scales; ·and I seemed to hear a voice shout from among the four animals and say, "A ration of corn for a day's wages, and three rations of barley for a day's wages, but do not tamper with the oil or the wine."

⁷ When he broke the fourth seal, I heard the ⁸ voice of the fourth animal shout, "Come." ·Immediately another horse appeared, deathly pale, and its rider was called Plague, and Hades followed at his heels.

They were given authority over a quarter of the earth, to kill by the sword, by famine, by plague and wild beasts.

⁹ When he broke the fifth seal, I saw underneath the altar the souls of all the people who had been killed on account of the word of God, for wit- ¹⁰ nessing to it. ·They shouted aloud, "Holy, faithful Master, how much longer will you wait before you pass sentence and take vengeance for our ¹¹ death on the inhabitants of the earth?" ·Each of them was given a white robe, and they were told to be patient a little longer, until the roll was com-

plete and their fellow servants and brothers had
been killed just as they had been.
12   In my vision, when he broke the sixth seal,
there was a violent earthquake and the sun went
as black as coarse sackcloth; the moon turned red
13 as blood all over, ·and the stars of the sky fell on
to the earth like figs dropping from a fig tree when
14 a high wind shakes it; ·the sky disappeared like
a scroll rolling up and all the mountains and is-
15 lands were shaken from their places. ·Then all the
earthly rulers, the governors and the command-
ers, the rich people and the men of influence, the
whole population, slaves and citizens, took to the
mountains to hide in caves and among the rocks.
16 They said to the mountains and the rocks, "Fall
on us and hide us away from the One who sits on
17 the throne and from the anger of the Lamb. ·For
the Great Day of his anger has come, and who
can survive it?"

☩

Obviously the second-, third-, and fourth-seal visions
symbolize the destructive powers of internal strife and
civil war, inflation and famine that devastate especially
the poor, and, finally, pestilence and death, the sum of
all oppressive powers. However, the meaning of the
first seal is debated. Because 19:11 ff describes the
Parousia-Christ in a similar fashion, some scholars suggest that it is the victorious Christ who opens the sequence of the seals. Others point to Mark 13:10 and
interpret the first rider as the Gospel conquering the
whole world. However, the meaning of the other seals
points to a different interpretation. Moreover, the repeated stress that divine permission was granted speaks
against such a positive interpretation of the first rider.
The first rider is clearly pictured as the victorious

military commander-in-chief riding in a triumphal procession. The bow, the sign of military prowess, points not only to the Parthians but also to the Babylonians. According to Jeremiah 51:56, Babylon's warriors are taken captive, their bows are broken. In the symbolic language of Revelation the bow therefore seems to express the expansionistic military power of Babylon/ Rome. As such, the first rider clearly is the anti-image of the victorious Parousia-Christ. The first four seals then do not portray a sequence of events but different aspects of Roman power and rule: the expansionistic military success of the Roman empire, the inner strife and war undermining the worldwide peace wrought by Augustus (pax Augusta), the concomitant inflation that deprives especially the poor of their essential food sustenance, and finally pestilence and death as bitter consequences of imperialistic war, civil battle, and epidemic hunger. In sum, the first four riders embody the sufferings of the endtime that was inaugurated with the death and resurrection of Christ. They are set in motion by the Lamb who is the agent opening the seals. Yet John does not thereby say that these calamities are willed by God and by Christ but only that they are tolerated and permitted as the repeated passive-apocalyptic expression "it was given" underlines.

The fifth seal (6:9–11) uses sacrificial terms to describe the Christians who were slaughtered and killed because of their witness to God and Christ. They ask the key question of people who suffer unbearable injustice and oppression: How long, O Lord? They ask the centuries-old question of those who suffer for God's cause and justice: When, O God, will you vindicate our faith and restore justice before those who oppress and persecute us in the whole world? Since many exegetes do not suffer unbearable oppression and are not driven by the question for justice, they often label this outcry as un-Christian and contrary to the preaching of the Gospel. However, only if this outcry for justice and for vindication, for the revenge of so many lives taken, and for so much blood unnecessarily shed is understood can the theological quest of Revelation be adjudicated. The Jewish historian Josephus reports that the Zealots endured torture and execution rather than acknowledge the Roman emperor as "sovereign." In using this title here for God, John alludes to the fact that those whom Roman justice has failed and killed acknowledge God as their true sovereign.

They are given white robes as a sign that they will participate in the marriage feast of the Lamb (cf. 1:8). At the same time they are told that they have to wait only a short time until the number of their partners and comrades who still have to suffer death is complete. The length of the short time or the "delay of the Parousia" is not yet established but depends on the Christians' decision for martyrdom. The death and suffering of the slaughtered Christians can be vindicated only by the final judgment because only then will the injustice of the present political powers be revealed and avenged. While Revelation 6:9–11 voices the outcry of the slaughtered for justice and retribution and 16:5–7 and 18:20 confirm that this outcry was heard and acted upon, 20:4–6 stresses the effect of the judgment of God for those killed: They will take part in the first resurrection and actively participate in the messianic reign.

The opening of the seals reaches its climax in the sixth seal that describes the "Day of the Lord" in terms of vast catastrophes and natural cataclysms. The portents in the heavens are so terrible that they can only

be understood in apocalyptic terms as the final dissolution of the whole world. The language and imagery is
not descriptive but hyperbolic. The apocalyptic language of cosmic cataclysms impresses on the reader
how terrible the wrath of God and the Lamb will be.
While the first four seals indicate the destructive
powers of the eschatological time of tribulation, the
sixth seal describes their judgment and punishment:
The kings and powerful leaders of the earth, the generals and the rich now hide before the wrath of the
Enthroned. Thus this seal is quite different from the
preceding ones which describe the political, economic,
and religious oppression characterizing the endtime.

The pattern of the seven seals is thus clearly defined
by early Christian apocalyptic belief and concepts. The
Christians are convinced that they live in "the last
days" and that with the death and resurrection of
Christ the final eschatological time has been inaugurated. Therefore, it is the exalted and victorious Lamb
who breaks the "seals" and sets the endtime events in
motion. According to the Synoptic apocalypse (Mk 13
parallels) the endtime has two periods or stages of development. After the "great tribulation" comes the
Parousia of Christ and the "Day of the Lord." They are
inaugurated and surrounded by earthquakes, portents in
heaven, cosmic cataclysms, and the final dissolution of
the world. As the short time before the cataclysmic
cosmic-end events, the time of suffering and tribulation
is characterized not only by wars, insurrections, fam-
ines, and pestilence but also by the persecution of the
elect, the appearance of false prophets and false
Christs who can do miraculous deeds, and the preaching of the Gospel. Most of these upheavals and events
are mentioned in the first five seals. While the experience of suffering and oppression is understood as a sign

that the Christians live in the last days, the cosmic-
cataclysmic events are wrought by God in vindication
for the suffering of the righteous and as punishment of
all oppressive, dehumanizing powers. This distinction of
the two periods of the endtime is important if we want
to understand the different functions of the seal septet
on the one hand and that of the bowl and trumpets on
the other.

STUDY QUESTIONS: D. H. Lawrence has called the book
of Revelation the "Judas in the New
Testament" because it asks for revenge and punishment. What do
you think of this evaluation? Is the
outcry for justice and vindication
incompatible with Christian love?

… … … … … … …

Revelation 7:1–8:1

THE ESCHATOLOGICAL PROTECTION
AND SALVATION OF THE ELECT

In structure and content, chapter 7 interrupts the seal septet insofar as it retards the opening of the last seal and keeps the reader in suspense. This interval or interlude does not speak of the sufferings of the endtime but discloses the divine protection and salvation of those "who stand firm to the end" (cf. Mk 13:13). The two visionary sections of chapter 7 are best understood when related to the two periods of the endtime symbolized by the opening of the preceding six seals. Revelation 7:1–8 seems to provide an answer to the concluding question of the sixth-seal vision: Who is able to be saved from the wrath and cosmic cataclysms of the Lord's Day? (cf. 6:17). Revelation 7:9–17 in turn pictures those who have "come out of the great tribulation" (7:14) that was revealed by the opening of the first five seals. Structurally it is significant that the vision and audition of 7:9–12 receive an explicit and extensive interpretation (7:13–17) that is paralleled only by the long explanation (17:7–18) of Babylon the Great, drunk with the blood of the saints (17:1–6).

¹ 7 Next I saw four angels, standing at the four
corners of the earth, holding the four winds
of the world back to keep them from blowing
² over the land or the sea or in the trees. ·Then I
saw another angel rising where the sun rises, car-
rying the seal of the living God; he called in a
powerful voice to the four angels whose duty was
³ to devastate land and sea, ·"Wait before you do
any damage on land or at sea or to the trees, until
we have put the seal on the foreheads of the ser-
⁴ vants of our God." ·Then I heard how many were
sealed: a hundred and forty-four thousand, out of
all the tribes of Israel.

⁵ From the tribe of Judah, twelve thousand had
been sealed; from the tribe of Reuben, twelve
thousand; from the tribe of Gad, twelve thou-
⁶ sand; ·from the tribe of Asher, twelve thousand;
from the tribe of Naphtali, twelve thousand; from
⁷ the tribe of Manasseh, twelve thousand; ·from the
tribe of Simeon, twelve thousand; from the tribe
of Levi, twelve thousand; from the tribe of Is-
⁸ sachar, twelve thousand; ·from the tribe of Zebu-
lun, twelve thousand; from the tribe of Joseph,
twelve thousand; and from the tribe of Benjamin,
twelve thousand were sealed.

⁹ After that I saw a huge number, impossible to
count, of people from every nation, race, tribe
and language; they were standing in front of the
throne and in front of the Lamb, dressed in white
robes and holding palms in their hands. They
¹⁰ shouted aloud, ·"Victory to our God, who sits on
¹¹ the throne, and to the Lamb!" ·And all the angels
who were standing in a circle round the throne,
surrounding the elders and the four animals, prostrated themselves before the throne, and touched
the ground with their foreheads, worshiping God
¹² with these words, "Amen. Praise and glory and
wisdom and thanksgiving and honor and power

and strength to our God for ever and ever. Amen."

13 One of the elders then spoke, and asked me, "Do you know who these people are, dressed in white robes, and where they have come from?"

14 I answered him, "You can tell me, my lord." Then he said, "These are the people who have been through the great persecution, and because they have washed their robes white again in the

15 blood of the Lamb, ·they now stand in front of God's throne and serve him day and night in his sanctuary; and the One who sits on the throne

16 will spread his tent over them. ·They will never hunger or thirst again; neither the sun nor scorch-

17 ing wind will ever plague them, ·because the Lamb who is at the throne will be their shepherd and will lead them to springs of living water; and God will wipe away all tears from their eyes."

18 The Lamb then broke the seventh seal, and there was silence in heaven for about half an hour.

✠

While the vision of 7:1–8 responds to the question who can survive the wrath of God and the Lamb, the second vision and its interpretation point to those who have "endured to the end" and therefore participate in the eschatological salvation.

First, in Old Testament and apocalyptic literature the four winds are the destructive agents of God, e.g., according to Jeremiah 49:36, the four winds carry out Yahweh's verdict against Elam. In Daniel 7:2, the four winds send forth the four terrible beasts on their destructive mission. In Revelation 7, the four winds clearly are destructive powers, but their action is retarded until the servants of God are sealed.

The sealing action could have several reference points and the complexity of allusion promotes a rich imagery. The sealing could refer to the names of the twelve tribes on the breastplate of the Jewish high priest, to the custom of wearing phylacteries, to the branding of a slave, to Christian baptism, to the protective mark of Ezekiel 9, to the bloodmark of the Exodus Lamb, to the oriental custom of marking one's belongings with the seal of one's ring, or to all of these. That the sealing is a sign of protection in the cataclysmic events of the cosmic plagues is supported by 9:4. The eschatological plagues kill only those who do not have the seal of God. It is often argued that the sealing does not mean protection of the Christians from suffering because they are called to endure sufferings and death. Such an objection, however, overlooks that the sealing does not protect from the sufferings of the "great tribulation" caused by the evil powers presented in the first five seals. It protects from the wrath of God and of the Lamb. The Christians are marked and thus protected from the eschatological cataclysms. Thus it is similar to the mark with the blood of the paschal lamb that protected the houses of the Israelites from the Exodus-plagues and initiated the liberation of Israel.

A great deal has been written about the identity of the 144,000 members of the tribes of Israel who receive the seal, especially since they seem to be contrasted to the great multitude coming from all nations in 7:9. The 144,000 represent an immense but definite number. Therefore, it is argued that they are the martyrs who are saved. However, the vision of the 144,000 clearly refers to people on earth and not to the eschatological bliss of the elect. Another interpretation suggests that they are the Jewish Christians

who have remained faithful in distinction to the gentile
Christians symbolized by the great multitude. Here
again the vision of the sealing does not refer to eschatological salvation but to protection during the turmoils
of the Last Day. Moreover, in New Testament times
the twelve tribes of Israel were not a historical but a
theological entity because only two tribes were still in
existence. Since their restitution was expected for the
eschatological endtime, the early Christians could understand themselves as the new "Israel of God" (Ga
6:16). Therefore, the Epistle of James, written to
Christians scattered in the Roman empire, can address
them as the "twelve tribes in the dispersion." Like 1
Peter, Revelation applies Exodus 19:5-6 to the Christian community and thus characterizes it as the new
people of God. Therefore, it is likely that the twelve
tribes signify in Revelation 7 the eschatologically re-
stored New Israel, the church. The 144,000 are those
Christians who are living at the time of the terrible cosmic dissolutions expressing the wrath of God and of
the Lamb. It is therefore interesting that the tribes of
Dan and Ephraim are not mentioned here. Both tribes
were infamous for their idolatry. The 144,000 are
those who are alive on the "Day of the Lord" and have
had no connection with idolatry or the anti-Christ.

The *second* vision pictures a great international multitude clad in white, with palms of victory in their
hands, proclaiming and praising the salvation (not victory) belonging to God and the Lamb. The Greek
word *soteria* means the total well-being of people.
The official source of such a total well-being, peace,
and salvation was supposed to be the Roman emperor.
Here those who stand before the throne acknowledge
God and the Lamb as the ultimate sources of all well-

being and salvation. The response of all the heavenly
world confirms this acclamation of the eschatological
elect with Amen and a hymn similar to those of chapters 4 and 5. The royal throne room, the heavenly temple, and the eschatological New Jerusalem are here
projected into one entity as the new world of total salvation and well-being in the presence of God and
Christ.

The vision receives a lengthy interpretation, a literary device of the author to underline the importance of
the vision. Whereas the 144,000 symbolize the Christians living and protected in the last days of cosmic
dissolution, the international multitude before the
throne are those who have endured and "survived" the
great tribulations preceding the final dissolution of the
Lord's Day. The time of eschatological tribulation is
the present time of the Asian communities, since in 1:9
John has stressed that, as their comrade, he shares in
the "tribulation." The sufferings of this time symbolized in the first five seals are understood in the Synoptic apocalypse Mark 13 parallels as the birth pangs
of a new world free from evil. The paradoxical image
that they have washed their robes in the blood of the
Lamb refers probably to baptism but also to their active
participation in the sufferings and violence of the anti-
human and antidivine powers that have wrought the
violent death of Christ. Their number therefore is not
necessarily limited to Christians but could be inclusive
of all those who have suffered the violence of the great
tribulation, war, hunger, pestilence, death, and persecution.

Their eschatological salvation and well-being are
proclaimed from the perspective of God and from a
human perspective. The Shekina-radiance of God's

presence in the midst of the people of God, who worship and acclaim the Enthroned, is symbolized by the "tent" that will be spread upon them. The total well-being and salvation of the people of God are pictured in colors and tones derived from the prophetic promises to the exiles of Israel returning from Babylon. Those who participate in the eschatological salvation will never again experience physical hardship, deprivation, hunger, or thirst. As their shepherd and ruler, Christ will satisfy them with the wellsprings of eternal life. All suffering, tears, and mourning will be wiped out. According to Revelation, final salvation does not just pertain to the soul and spiritual realities. It is the abolishment of all dehumanization and suffering and at the same time the fullness of human well-being. The vision and promise of such ultimate well-being are thus clearly intended as a rectification of the great tribulation with its sufferings of war, peacelessness, hunger, and inflation, pestilence, persecution, and death. The outcry of those who asked for justice and revenge of their lives is granted in this vision of eschatological well-being and salvation.

After the interludes of chapter 7 envisioning the eschatological protection and salvation of the people of God, the opening of the seventh seal is almost anticlimactic. It is, however, a brilliant literary device for provoking a striking contrast and deepening suspense. The half hour of breathless silence impressively contrasts with the acclamation and hymn of chapter 7 as well as with the deafening noise of the thunders, voices, and earthquakes of 8:5. At the same time it implies structurally that the blowing of the seven trumpets is prepared during this interval of silence and therefore develops the content of the scroll whose seals are now opened.

STUDY QUESTIONS: What is your understanding and vision of eschatological well-being and bliss? Why is it important to have such a vision when involved in the struggle against oppressive social, political, and religious powers? Can those who are not involved in such a struggle understand such a vision?

Revelation 8:2–9:21
SIX TRUMPETS ANNOUNCING
THE ESCHATOLOGICAL PLAGUES

The literary structure of the trumpet septet parallels that of the seals. Like the first four seals, the first four trumpets follow a definite, parallel pattern, whereas the fifth and sixth trumpets correspond in form to the fifth and sixth seals insofar as they do not follow the same pattern but are greatly expanded. The proclamation of the woes by the eagle, or vulture, clearly marks this formal break in the trumpet series. As the interlude of chapter 7 retarded the opening of the seventh seal, so does the interlude of chapters 10–11 delay the victory blast of the seventh trumpet.

The artful composition of the whole section can be even better grasped when we recognize the author's literary technique of intercalation, sandwiching, or interlocking. The author employs the method of intercalation in the following way: He narrates two episodes or two formal units (A and A') that essentially belong together. Between these two units, he intercalates another unit different in form and content from the other two (B). We have seen that, e.g., in structuring the introduction of the book the author uses this method of inclusion, by inserting the epistolary form into the prophetic form of introduction. In a simi-

lar way the author intercalates the heavenly liturgy
8:3–5 (B) between the appearance of the angels with
the trumpets 8:2 (A) and the execution of the plagues
(A').

At the same time he interlinks the trumpets with the
following visions by way of a double intercalation. Revelation 10:1–11:14 is clearly marked as an interlude
inserted into the septet of the trumpets (8:6–9:21a;
10:1–11:14b; 11:15–19a'). At the same time 10:1–
11:14 belongs to the following chapters 12–14 since
it refers to the same time period and the same persecution by the beast. By characterizing this unit as
"little scroll" the author parallelizes it to, and includes
it into, the scroll taken over by the Lamb. The small
prophetic scroll thus follows the same pattern of inclusion (10:1–11:14a; 11:15–19b; 12:12–14a'). Moreover, the woe pronouncement of the vulture ties it
also to the trumpet visions insofar as the first woe is
announced as having passed in 9:12, the second in
11:14, and the third as referring to chapters 12–13 in
12:12a. All three woes refer to the demonic and sa-
tanic evil powers.

What is the literary function of the trumpet visions
within the overall context of Revelation? Chapter 5,
verse 1, stresses that the scroll had writings "inside and
on the back." After the Lamb has opened the seals and
the endtime has been inaugurated, the content of the
scroll can be acted out. Since the trumpet and bowl visions recall the pattern of the Egyptian plagues and
parallel each other, they seem to represent the two
written sides of the scroll. As becomes clear in the
bowl septet, they execute the wrath and judgment of
God. As the Egyptian plagues were inflicted in order to
make possible the Exodus of Israel from Egypt, so the
cosmic plagues of the trumpets and bowls execute the

judgment of God over the cosmos, indicating the liberation of the New Israel from the oppression of Babylon/Rome.

2 Next I saw seven trumpets being given to the seven angels who stand in the presence of God.
3 Another angel, who had a golden censer, came and stood at the altar. A large quantity of incense was given to him to offer with the prayers of all the saints on the golden altar that stood in front
4 of the throne; ·and so from the angel's hand the smoke of the incense went up in the presence of
5 God and with it the prayers of the saints. ·Then the angel took the censer and filled it with the fire from the altar, which he then threw down on to the earth; immediately there came peals of thunder and flashes of lightning, and the earth shook.
6 The seven angels that had the seven trumpets
7 now made ready to sound them. ·The first blew his trumpet and, with that, hail and fire, mixed with blood, were dropped on the earth; a third of the earth was burned up, and a third of all trees,
8 and every blade of grass was burned. ·The second angel blew his trumpet, and it was as though a great mountain, all on fire, had been dropped into
9 the sea: a third of the sea turned into blood, ·a third of all the living things in the sea were killed,
10 and a third of all ships were destroyed. ·The third angel blew his trumpet, and a huge star fell from the sky, burning like a ball of fire, and it fell on a
11 third of all rivers and springs; ·this was the star called Wormwood, and a third of all water turned to bitter wormwood, so that many people died
12 from drinking it. ·The fourth angel blew his trumpet, and a third of the sun and a third of the moon and a third of the stars were blasted, so that the light went out of a third of them and for a third of the day there was no illumination, and the same with the night.

13   In my vision, I heard an eagle, calling aloud as it flew high overhead, "Trouble, trouble, trouble, for all the people on earth at the sound of the other three trumpets which the three angels are going to blow."

1   9 Then the fifth angel blew his trumpet, and I saw a star that had fallen from heaven on to the earth, and he was given the key to the shaft
2   leading down to the Abyss. ·When he unlocked the shaft of the Abyss, smoke poured up out of the Abyss like the smoke from a huge furnace so that the sun and the sky were darkened by it,
3   and out of the smoke dropped locusts which were given the powers that scorpions have on the earth:
4   they were forbidden to harm any fields or crops or trees and told only to attack any men who were
5   without God's seal on their foreheads. ·They were not to kill them, but to give them pain for five months, and the pain was to be the pain of a
6   scorpion's sting. ·When this happens, men will long for death and not find it anywhere; they will want to die and death will evade them.

7   To look at, these locusts were like horses armored for battle; they had things that looked like gold crowns on their heads, and faces that seemed
8   human, ·and hair like women's hair, and teeth
9   like lions' teeth. ·They had body-armor like iron breastplates, and the noise of their wings sounded like a great charge of horses and chariots into bat-
10   tle. ·Their tails were like scorpions', with stings, and it was with them that they were able to injure
11   people for five months. ·As their leader they had their emperor, the angel of the Abyss, whose name in Hebrew is Abaddon, or Apollyon in Greek.

12   That was the first of the troubles; there are still two more to come.

13   The sixth angel blew his trumpet, and I heard a voice come out of the four horns of the golden
14   altar in front of God. ·It spoke to the sixth angel with the trumpet, and said, "Release the four angels that are chained up at the great river Euphra-

15 tes." ·These four angels had been put there ready
for this hour of this day of this month of this year,
and now they were released to destroy a third of
16 the human race. ·I learned how many there were
in their army: twice ten thousand times ten thou-
17 sand mounted men. ·In my vision I saw the
horses, and the riders with their breastplates of
flame color, hyacinth-blue and sulphur-yellow;
the horses had lions' heads, and fire, smoke and
18 sulphur were coming out of their mouths. ·It was
by these three plagues, the fire, the smoke and the
sulphur coming out of their mouths, that the one
19 third of the human race was killed. ·All the
horses' power was in their mouths and their tails:
their tails were like snakes, and had heads that
20 were able to wound. ·But the rest of the human
race, who escaped these plagues, refused either to
abandon the things they had made with their own
hands—the idols made of gold, silver, bronze,
stone and wood that can neither see nor hear nor
21 move—or to stop worshiping devils. ·Nor did they
give up their murdering, or witchcraft, or fornication or stealing.

✠

The prelude 8:2–5 introduces the seven angels of
the Presence or the seven archangels who are probably
identical with the angels pouring out the bowls of the
wrath of God. The trumpets, which are given to
them, evoke many symbolic allusions: Trumpets were
sounded to announce war and victory, to call people
together, to celebrate feast days, or to herald the coro-
nation of a king. Here they call to mind especially the
eschatological connotations given in the Old Testament
and New Testament with the sound of trumpets: They
herald the Day of the Lord (Zp 1:14 ff), announce the

day of judgment (2 Ezr 6:23), or herald the resurrection of the dead and the dawn of a new order (cf. 1 Th 4:16; 1 Co 15:52; Mt 24:31).

After the introduction of the seven trumpet angels, the interlude 8:3–5 focuses our attention on the heavenly liturgy of wrath and judgment. A priest-angel adds incense to the prayers of the saints upon the golden altar which was before the throne of God. The prayers of the saints are here likened to burning charcoal upon which the grains of incense are laid so that the smoke goes up before God's throne. Whereas in 5:8 the prayers of the saints are symbolized by bowls of incense used in the hymnic liturgy acknowledging the Lamb's enthronement to kingship, here the prayers of the saints kindle and sustain the fire of the altar that symbolizes God's wrath and judgment. Like the outcry of the martyrs in 6:9–11, so the prayers of the saints, who are persecuted, demand justice and foster the judgment of God.

The first four trumpet visions (8:6–12) are, in form, parallel to the first four seal visions but in content quite different. They bring destruction to all four elements of the cosmos. The symbol of fire that is found in all four visions is the same fire that the priest-angel has cast down on earth. It is a sign of the wrath and judgment of God. This judgment of God affects the whole cosmos, the earth, the sea, the inland waters, and the heavenly bodies. However, the destruction of the four dimensions of the world is not total since the plagues of the trumpets destroy only one third of it. Those who have the protection of God's seal will not be touched by the cosmic plagues just as the Israelites were spared from them.

The fifth- and the sixth-trumpet visions are distinct in structure and in content. They do not enact the destruction of the cosmic order. Instead, they reveal the activity of the demonic-satanic power, which tortures and kills a third of humanity. Whereas the fifth trumpet is clearly identical with the first woe, it is debated whether the second woe is identical with the events told in 9:13–11:14, or only with the vision of the two prophets in 11:3–14.

The fifth trumpet (9:1–12) evokes the repulsive image of mythical locusts coming from the abyss, which was opened by the angel-star fallen like Satan from heaven (cf. Lk 10:18). The plague of the locusts that have the power of scorpions is derived from Exodus 10:1–20, which had been already eschatologically interpreted as a portent of the destruction coming with the dawn of the Day of the Lord (1:2–2:11). The bizarre description of the locust as horse-shaped, long-haired flying insects with scorpion tails, wearing golden crowns above human faces which are marred by lions' teeth should not be allegorized but perceived as a repulsive image of unnatural, demonic power. The Greek name of their king Apollyon is probably a derogatory wordplay on the god Apollo, since the locust was one of his symbols and Domitian claimed to be an incarnation of this god. If such a pun was intended, then Revelation ironically claims that the destructive host of the abyss has as its king the Roman emperor who claims to be divine.

The sixth-trumpet plague (9:13–21) introduces an even more cruel and repulsive picture. The torment of the locusts gives way to the massacre of one third of all human beings by fire-breathing mythological horse-monsters. The introductory reference to the golden altar alludes to the heavenly liturgy of judgment, and the reference to the four angels recalls the staying of the four destructive winds in 7:1–3. The four angels are loosed here in order to kill one third of the world's population. Their task is accomplished by a double myriad of myriads cavalry. The plague is not executed by the riders but by the horses out of whose mouths fire, smoke, and brimstone issue to kill. Whereas the power to kill is in the mouths of these mythic monsterlike horses, their serpent tails have the power to harm. However, the concluding verses 20-21 indicate that John tells this grotesque and brutal vision not for cruelty's sake but in order to call to repentance. Yet in line with the pattern of the Egyptian plagues, it is stressed that those who were not killed did not repent their idolatry and the pagan practices connected with it.

The description of these last two plague visions indicates how disastrous it would be if we would misunderstand Revelation as a description or prediction of events which have happened or will happen literally. Revelation is neither an accurate transcription of divine revelation nor a factual prediction of future eschatological events. It is a literary work of vision written in the language of image and myth. As such, it could be likened to contemporary literary science fiction. The futuristic accounts of atomic warfare, ecological devastation, or scientific cloning are not predictions or accurate descriptions of what must come, but poetic imagination of what might come if the industrialized nations do not stop their military expansion or their technological exploitation of the earth. These terrible visions of a manipulative and dehumanized future seek to shock us out of our own present lethargy. They are based on our knowledge of the destructive possibilities of nuclear power and draw out the worst possibilities of destruction so that we may reconsider our present military spending or nuclear development. In a similar fashion, John puts before us the repulsive and grotesque powers of Satan and the abyss in order to shock the reader into repentance from idolatry or to recall trust and confidence in God's humanizing power despite all evidence to the contrary.

STUDY QUESTIONS: Why does John develop such a gruesome and mythological picture of the judgments of God? What is the function of the repulsive images presented especially in the fifth- and sixth-trumpet visions?

D. *The Prophetic Community and Its Oppressors*
Revelation 10:1 to 15:4

INTRODUCTION

Anyone attempting to construct a chronological or even a logical sequence of events in Revelation has to give up in despair when analyzing the central chapters of the book. Whereas the seven cycles of the messages, seals, and trumpets at least have followed an obvious numerical pattern and evolved from each other, no such pattern is apparent in Revelation 10:1–14:20. Several scholars have attempted to establish a seven series of unnumbered visions, but their proposals differ widely. Against such reconstructions is also the observation that the author would have been capable of writing another seven series in clear and explicit fashion were that his intention.

Since John did not employ the literary technique of numerical structure in Revelation 10:1–14:20, we must pay special attention to other literary means which are also employed elsewhere in Revelation. Such literary techniques are those of intercalation or inclusion, cross-reference, and symbolic contrasts. The characterization and dramatic introduction of the little scroll in 10:1 ff clearly intends to parallel this open scroll with the sevenfold sealed scroll of chapter 5. Moreover, the prophetic commissioning and the characterization of the angel in 10:1 ff refer the reader back to the inaugural vision and its prophetic call in chapter

1. Last and most important, the references to the beast and its mark (11:7; 13:1; 13:16 f; 14:9; 15:2 cf; also 14:1), and to the duration of the activity of the Christians and their oppressors (11:2,3; 12:15; 13:6), cover the same time period. Moreover, the contrasts of the beast and the Lamb, or of the beastly homage and the divine liturgy, indicate that chapters 11–14 are dominated by the same actors. The sevenfold sealed scroll taken over by the Lamb represents the eschatological endtime tribulation and the final cataclysms of the Lord's Day from a "heavenly perspective." The open little scroll taken and eaten by John, in turn, draws our attention to the situation of oppression on earth. This earthly focus of the following visions that tell about the eschatological struggle of the followers of the Lamb with the idolatrous and destructive powers of the beast might be one of the reasons why John does not communicate these visions in the form of a septet since the number seven is the number of perfection, whereas the number of the beast is 666.

As I have already pointed out, the little prophetic scroll is literarily interconnected with the preceding section of the trumpets by means of an intercalation and double inclusion. Chapters 10 and 11 are clearly marked as an interlude before the blast of the last trumpet and as such they have the same structural position within Revelation as the interludes of chapter 7. At the same time they refer to the same situation and time as chapters 12–14, to which they are a prelude. Thus the following double inclusion can be recognized: a (sixth trumpet), b (interlude of chs. 10 and 11), a' (seventh trumpet), and b' (chs. 12–13).

The conclusion of the little scroll is also interrelated with the following bowl visions by way of intercalation and inclusion. The vision of the 144,000 on Mount

Sion (14:1–5:a) is followed by the announcement of the bowl septet and the destruction of Babylon (14:6–13:b) and complemented by the vision of the double eschatological harvest (14:14–20:a′) which in turn leads to the presentation of the seven angels with the bowls of God's wrath (15:1:b′). The visions of chapters 11–14 climax in the heavenly homage to God's justice by the victors (15:2–3:a″) that is, at the same time, a prelude and interpretation of the last cosmic plagues septet (15:6 ff:b″). Then the central section of Revelation can be diagrammed as follows: C(9:13–21);   D(10:1–11:14);   C(11:15–19); D(12:1–14:5);   C′(14:6–13);   D(14:14–20); C′(15:1); D(15:2–5); C′(15:6 ff). (See outline in Appendix.) Such an analysis of the structural sequence is important because it sheds light on the structural and thereby also theological function of the individual sections.

Revelation 10:1–11:13
THE SELF-UNDERSTANDING
AND TASK OF THE CHRISTIAN
PROPHET

The interlude Revelation 10:1–11:13 is marked not only structurally as a single vision but also stylistically insofar as the "I saw" of 10:1 introduces the whole section. It is therefore misleading to accept the present chapter division, especially since the enumeration of verses and chapters was only added at a much later date. The single vision of the trumpet interlude can be divided into the following sections: the angel and the thunders (10:1–4), the oath of the angel referring to the seventh trumpet (10:5–7), the taking and eating of the little scroll (10:8–10), the renewed prophetic commissioning of John (10:11–11:2), the power and fate of the two witnesses (11:3–12), and finally a summary statement about the effects of the whole vision (11:13–14).

¹ **10** Then I saw another powerful angel coming down from heaven, wrapped in a cloud, with a rainbow over his head; his face was
² like the sun, and his legs were pillars of fire. ·In his hand he had a small scroll, unrolled; he put

his right foot in the sea and his left foot on the
³ land ·and he shouted so loud, it was like a lion
roaring. At this, seven claps of thunder made
⁴ themselves heard ·and when the seven thunderclaps had spoken, I was preparing to write, when
I heard a voice from heaven say to me, "Keep the
words of the seven thunderclaps secret and do not
⁵ write them down." ·Then the angel that I had
seen, standing on the sea and the land, raised his
⁶ right hand to heaven, ·and swore by the One who
lives for ever and ever, and made heaven and all
that is in it, and earth and all it bears, and the sea
⁷ and all it holds, "The time of waiting is over; ·at
the time when the seventh angel is heard sounding his trumpet, God's secret intention will be
fulfilled, just as he announced in the Good News
told to his servants the prophets."

⁸   Then I heard the voice I had heard from
heaven speaking to me again. "Go," it said "and
take that open scroll out of the hand of the angel
⁹ standing on sea and land." ·I went to the angel
and asked him to give me the small scroll, and he
said, "Take it and eat it; it will turn your stomach
sour, but in your mouth it will taste as sweet as
¹⁰ honey." ·So I took it out of the angel's hand, and
swallowed it; it was as sweet as honey in my
mouth, but when I had eaten it my stomach
¹¹ turned sour. ·Then I was told, "You are to prophesy again, this time about many different nations
and countries and languages and emperors."

¹ **11** Then I was given a long cane as a measuring rod, and I was told, "Go and measure God's sanctuary, and the altar, and the people
² who worship there; ·but leave out the outer court
and do not measure it, because it has been handed
over to pagans—they will trample on the holy city
³ for forty-two months. ·But I shall send my two
witnesses to prophesy for those twelve hundred
⁴ and sixty days, wearing sackcloth. ·These are the
two olive trees and the two lamps that stand be-
⁵ fore the Lord of the world. ·Fire can come from
their mouths and consume their enemies if any-

one tries to harm them; and if anybody does try
to harm them he will certainly be killed in this
⁶ way. ·They are able to lock up the sky so that it
does not rain as long as they are prophesying;
they are able to turn water into blood and strike
the whole world with any plague as often as they
⁷ like. ·When they have completed their witnessing,
the beast that comes out of the Abyss is going to
make war on them and overcome them and kill
⁸ them. ·Their corpses will lie in the main street
of the Great City known by the symbolic names
Sodom and Egypt, in which their Lord was cru-
⁹ cified. ·Men out of every people, race, language
and nation will stare at their corpses, for three-
¹⁰ and-a-half days, not letting them be buried, ·and
the people of the world will be glad about it and
celebrate the event by giving presents to each
other, because these two prophets have been a
plague to the people of the world."
¹¹   After the three-and-a-half days, God breathed
life into them and they stood up, and everybody
¹² who saw it happen was terrified; ·then they heard
a loud voice from heaven say to them, "Come
up here," and while their enemies were watching,
¹³ they went up to heaven in a cloud. ·Immediately,
there was a violent earthquake, and a tenth of the
city collapsed; seven thousand persons were killed
in the earthquake, and the survivors, overcome
with fear, could only praise the God of heaven.

✠

1. 10:1–4 introduces the open little scroll that is,
however, not in the outstretched palm of God but in
that of a mighty angel whose appearance alludes to
some of the Christological features of the inaugural vision of 1:12–20. The downward movement of this
powerful angel focuses the seer's attention again on the
earth. The rainbow around the angel's head might be a

sign of God's covenant with creation (Gn 9:13), whereas the cloud and the pillars of fire evoke the Exodus and Sinai covenant (Ex 13:21 ff; 19:16 ff).

The seven thunders and the command to "seal up" what they have said have puzzled many minds and are far from being resolved. Thunder with lightning, etc., in Revelation expresses theophany (cf. 4:5; 8:5; 11:19; 16:18) or characterizes a heavenly voice (cf. 6:1; 14:2; 19:6). It is likely that Psalm 29 has influenced the symbol of the seven thunders since this psalm understands thunder as "the voice of God" and repeats this phrase seven times in developing the power and splendor of God's voice. But why must the seer seal what the sevenfold thundering voice of God has revealed? It is possible that John alludes here to a traditional Synoptic saying according to which only the Father knows the day or hour of the Parousia (Mk 13:32; Mt 24:36). The thunders and the prohibition to write are then literary means of stressing that no one can know the day and hour of the end.

2. This interpretation seems to be corroborated by the oath of the angel that "there should be no delay," but that at the sounding of the seventh trumpet the mystery of God should be fulfilled (10:5-7). This section has a literary backdrop (Dn 12:1-7). After Daniel is told to seal the book until the time of the end (12:4), someone asks: "How long until these wonders take place?" In response to this question, the angel swears by God who "lives forever" that "a time and two times and half a time" have to pass (cf. Rv 12:14) until "he who crushes the power of the holy people meets his end" (12:7). The same time period is mentioned in Revelation as the time of the church and the persecution of the beast. As we will see, the seventh

trumpet announces the theophany and acknowledg-
ment of God's empire over the whole world as the
mystery that was revealed as "good news" to the
prophets. Thus the expression mystery, the secret plan
or decree of God, might refer back to what the seven
thunders have revealed to John. When the seventh
trumpet is sounded, then this mystery of God will be
revealed. Since the seventh trumpet is already sounded
toward the center of the book, it is obvious that the sequence of the visions and chapters is not chronological.
The seventh trumpet speaks about the same eschatological salvation as the last chapters of Revelation
do.

3. After the pressing question "How long?" is
clarified, our attention is shifted back to the little scroll
upon the outstretched hand of the angel (11:8-10).
John is told to take and eat this scroll, i.e, to become
magically aware of its contents and internalize them.
As the "word of God," referring to God's eschatological salvation, the little scroll tastes sweet (cf. Ps
19:10) but becomes bitter when digested. At the blast
of the third trumpet, a third of the waters became bitter
"and many died of the water because it was made bitter." The bitter and poisonous water symbolizes death.
Similarly, the "turning bitter of the scroll" spells death.
The following chapter draws out the "sweetness" of the
prophetic word promising divine protection of the true
worshipers and, at the same time, announcing the "bitter truth" that the prophetic witnesses will be killed in
the war with the beast.

4. To this double taste of the small scroll corresponds the double commissioning of the prophet
(10:11-11:2). The injunction to prophesy against
many nations is phrased in the typical Danielic for-

mula, but the addition of "kings" indicates that the author has the following chapters in mind. While the nations rage against God and the true worshipers of God, the kings of the earth are the followers of the great city Babylon/Rome.

John's prophetic word is to be complemented by a prophetic sign-action that could be inspired by Ezekiel 40:3. However, in Ezekiel as in Revelation 21:15, the measuring of Jerusalem means restoration, whereas the action of John is usually interpreted as signifying protection. Many exegetes suggest that John incorporates here a zealotic oracle as his source that was a handout which had been distributed before the destruction of Jerusalem by the Romans. However, we must ask why John would have incorporated here such a propaganda handout if he is writing long after the destruction of Jerusalem *and* of the temple. The tradition which possibly was taken over here does not give us any inkling of the intended meaning in the context of Revelation.

The symbolic action of John, like that of the Old Testament prophets, has the function of dramatizing his prophetic announcements. This prophetic action must be understood in a symbolic-metaphorical way since the temple and the city of Jerusalem were in ruins. Like the measuring in Enoch 61:1–5, the measuring here probably symbolizes eschatological protection and strengthening. Those who are eschatologically protected are the priestly worshipers of God. In contrast to those Christians who are the true worshipers of God, the court of the Gentiles will not be protected but will be excluded from eschatological salvation. Revelation 11:2b seems to closely parallel Luke 21:24 but replaces the Lukan Jerusalem with the expression "holy city" and specifies the "time of the Gentiles" with the Danielic number "forty and two months."

Since the author uses the name Jerusalem only for the New Jerusalem, his characterization of the city as the "holy city" does not refer either to the eschatological nor to the historical Jerusalem that is identified with "the great city" (11:8). The holy city includes the same persons as the first characterizations "temple, Altar, worshipers" do, namely the Christian community. We thus can translate the symbolic language of 11:1-2: John is told to prophesy that as the true priestly worshipers the Christians will be eschatologically strengthened and protected, whereas the Gentiles are excluded from eschatological salvation (thrown outside, cf. Mt 8:12 and Rv 22:15). The reason for this is that they have persecuted the Christians during the endtime. Revelation 11:1-2 is therefore a prophetic announcement of reversal. While the Christians now suffer the oppressions and persecutions of the nations, they will be eschatologically protected, whereas the nations will experience the eschatological plagues and punishments of God's wrath.

5. The witness and fate of the Christian prophet are told in 11:3-12. Insofar as the vision of the two witnesses does not have its own introduction, this vision expands formally the commissioning vision of 10:11-11:2 and thus functions as an overture to the whole section. During the period when the church is downtrodden by the nations, the two witnesses function as eschatological prophets calling the peoples of the earth to repentance and penitence. Revelation 11:3-12 therefore seems to expand and elaborate the prophetic commissioning in 10:11 in a symbolical fashion. The

prophetic activity of the witnesses parallels the time of
the church's persecution.

After the power and duration of their activity are
announced (11:3), the identities of the two witnesses
are symbolically characterized (11:4), their power and
protection are elaborated (11:5–6), and their fate is
described in analogy to that of Christ (7–12). By referring to the two witnesses as two olive trees and
lampstands as well as by interpreting the great city
"spiritually," John indicates that he intentionally uses
symbolic-theological language. Any attempt to identify
the two witnesses with historical personages, or to interpret every feature of the vision in a historical-
allegorical way, is therefore inappropriate and cannot
lead to satisfactory results.

The images of olive tree and temple menorah refer
to Zechariah 4:2 where they symbolize the kingship of
Zerubbabel and the high priesthood of Joshua. The
temple menorah also refers back to the inaugural vision
where the interpretation of 1:20 identified it as a symbol of the Christian community. In 1:6 and 5:10 the
royal/priestly character of the Christians was stressed.
The number two reflects probably Deuteronomy 19:15
(cf. Jn 8:17) that at least two persons are needed
for valid witness, and Luke 10:1 where the disciples
are sent out in twos. That this passage was in the mind
of John is also indicated by the assertion that no one is
able to harm them because according to Luke 10:19
the disciples were promised that nothing would harm
them, not even serpents, scorpions and "all the power
of the enemy." The phrase also refers back to the
"measuring" of 11:1.

The royal/priestly witnesses are endowed with the
power of Elijah (fire from their mouths; power to shut
the sky) and Moses (power over the waters and refer-

ence to "every plague") who were expected to return as the eschatological prophets. The power of the Christian prophets and witnesses "to smite the earth with every plague" of course also refers to the influence of the Christians in bringing about the eschatological plagues (cf. the outcry of the witnesses for justice in 6:10 and the "prayer of the saints" in 5:8 and 8:2 ff). Although the Christians will be persecuted and oppressed, they are able to execute their prophetic witness and call to repentance. No harm will be done that could prohibit their activity, but what is done against them increases the wrath of God and the eschatological plagues.

The attempt to puzzle out each statement of 11:7–12 in an allegorical fashion has led to great exegetical confusion about the meaning of the text. However, the main lines of the picture are clear. The eschatological fate of the Christian prophets and witnesses is very much like that of "their Lord." After their task is fulfilled the beast ascending from the abyss (cf. 9:1; 13:1) will fight, conquer, and kill them (cf. 12:17; 13:7,15). Thus the vision of the two witnesses' activity is clearly identical or interlinked with the following visions of chapters 12–13. The expression "great city" that, according to prophetic (not allegorical) insight, is the moral and spiritual equivalent of Sodom and Egypt refers clearly to the oppressive power of Rome since the Romans were legally responsible for the execution of Jesus. Their death, resurrection, and exaltation mirror the fate of Jesus. Although the Christian prophets and witnesses are eschatologically protected and cannot be prohibited from the execution of their task, as did their Lord they will also suffer death. Yet they, too, are promised resurrection and exaltation.

6. The visions elaborating the task and witness of the Christian prophet conclude with a cosmic earthquake and the partial destruction of the city and its inhabitants. But while the cosmic plagues (6:12; 8:5; 11:19; 16:18) do not lead to repentance, the prophetic witness of the Christians until death does. Nine tenths of the nations or citizens of the Roman empire repent and "give God honor." Since Revelation is permeated with the preaching of wrath upon the citizens of the world, scholars argue that 11:13 does not suggest the repentance but only the fear of the nations. However, the expression "they praised the God of heaven" is repeated in 14:7 as the content of the Gospel announced to all the peoples of the earth. Moreover, 11:13 seems to foreshadow the pronouncement of 15:3–4 that all nations will come and worship God. Only when we acknowledge that Revelation hopes for the conversion of the nations, in response to the Christian witness and preaching, will we be able to see that it does not advocate a "theology of resentment" but a theology of justice.

STUDY QUESTION: Since the sequence of Revelation is not chronological but thematic and theological, it must be doubted that it is possible to reconstruct and to predict a revealed series of events which will happen before the end of the world. How would you communicate this insight to someone who understands Revelation to be the revealed calendar of the endtime events?

Revelation 11:14–19
THE SEVENTH TRUMPET:
THE ETERNAL KINGDOM
OF GOD AND CHRIST

14 That was the second of the troubles; the third is to come quickly after it.

15 Then the seventh angel blew his trumpet, and voices could be heard shouting in heaven, calling, "The kingdom of the world has become the kingdom of our Lord and his Christ, and he will reign for ever and ever." ·The twenty-four elders, en-

16 throned in the presence of God, prostrated themselves and touched the ground with their fore-

17 heads worshiping God ·with these words, "We give thanks to you, Almighty Lord God, He-Is-and-He-Was, for using your great power and be-

18 ginning your reign. ·The nations were seething with rage and now the time has come for your own anger, and for the dead to be judged, and for your servants the prophets, for the saints and for all who worship you, small or great, to be rewarded. The time has come to destroy those who are destroying the earth."

19 Then the sanctuary of God in heaven opened, and the ark of the covenant could be seen inside it. Then came flashes of lightning, peals of thunder and an earthquake, and violent hail.

✠

The statement of 11:14 refers us back to the fifth trumpet (cf. 9:12) and thus clearly characterizes structurally 10:1–11:13 as an interlude of the trumpet septet. At the same time, the seventh-trumpet vision functions as a prelude in the visionary series about the war of the beast against the saints. Finally, the oath of the angel in 10:5 ff has assured the reader that the seventh trumpet announces the end and final salvation. It thus corresponds to the visions in 21–22.

The judgment and reign of God and Christ are announced in the eschatological victory hymn 11:17–18. It punishes "the destroyers of the earth" and rewards not only the Christians but all those who have repented and acknowledged God. God's judgment and empire mean the liberation of the earth from all destructive powers, especially Rome (cf. 19:2), and the renewal of the covenant with creation. The wrath of the nations has provoked the wrath of God expressed in the eschatological plagues. But their execution leads to the liberation of all humanity and of the whole earth from oppressive and destructive powers. This is the hope that John places before the Christians who now have to suffer oppression and persecution by the nations.

STUDY QUESTION: Why is it important for the theological understanding of Revelation that the majority of humanity will positively respond to the Gospel of justice?

Revelation 12:1–17
THE WOMAN
AND THE DRAGON

The composition of chapter 12 has again the form of an inclusion. Between the great portent of the glorious woman and the powerful dragon (12:1–6) and the persecution of the woman by the dragon (12:13–17), the vision about war in heaven waged by the dragon is inserted (12:7–12). Our attention is drawn, at first, to the glorious sign in heaven, but at the end of each section our focus again shifts toward the earth. The whole vision seems to be a mythological elaboration of the eschatological war motif already sounded in 11:7.

1 2 Now a great sign appeared in heaven: a woman, adorned with the sun, standing on the moon, and with the twelve stars on her head
2 for a crown: ·She was pregnant, and in labor, cry-
3 ing aloud in the pangs of childbirth. ·Then a second sign appeared in the sky, a huge red dragon which had seven heads and ten horns, and each
4 of the seven heads crowned with a coronet. ·Its tail dragged a third of the stars from the sky and dropped them to the earth, and the dragon stopped in front of the woman as she was having the child, so that he could eat it as soon as it was

⁵ born from its mother. ·The woman brought a male child into the world, the son who was to rule all the nations with an iron sceptre, and the child was taken straight up to God and to his throne, ⁶ while the woman escaped into the desert, where God had made a place of safety ready, for her to be looked after in the twelve hundred and sixty days.

⁷ And now war broke out in heaven, when Michael with his angels attacked the dragon. The ⁸ dragon fought back with his angels, ·but they ⁹ were defeated and driven out of heaven. ·The great dragon, the primeval serpent, known as the devil or Satan, who had deceived all the world, was hurled down to the earth and his angels were ¹⁰ hurled down with him. ·Then I heard a voice shout from heaven, "Victory and power and empire for ever have been won by our God, and all authority for his Christ, now that the persecutor, who accused our brothers day and night before ¹¹ our God, has been brought down. ·They have triumphed over him by the blood of the Lamb and by the witness of their martyrdom, because even in the face of death they would not cling to ¹² life. ·Let the heavens rejoice and all who live there; but for you, earth and sea, trouble is coming—because the devil has gone down to you in a rage, knowing that his days are numbered."

¹³ As soon as the devil found himself thrown down to the earth, he sprang in pursuit of the woman, ¹⁴ the mother of the male child, ·but she was given a huge pair of eagle's wings to fly away from the serpent into the desert, to the place where she was to be looked after for a year and twice a year ¹⁵ and half a year. ·So the serpent vomited water from his mouth, like a river, after the woman, ¹⁶ to sweep her away in the current, ·but the earth came to her rescue; it opened its mouth and swallowed the river thrown up by the dragon's jaws.

¹⁷ Then the dragon was enraged with the woman and went away to make war on the rest of her

children, that is, all who obey God's commandments and bear witness for Jesus.

✠

The myth of the Queen of Heaven with the divine
child was internationally known at the time of John.
Variations of it are found in Babylonia, Egypt, Greece,
Asia Minor, and in astral religion. The elements of this
myth are: the goddess with the divine child, the great
red dragon and his enmity to mother and child; the
protection of mother and child are also incorporated in
Revelation 12. As in other versions of the myth, the
dragon seeks the child not yet born in order to devour
and kill him. The pregnant woman is pursued for the
child she carries. Whereas in other forms of the myth
she either is carried away to give birth in a protected
place or she gives birth in a miraculous way and es-
capes the onslaught of the dragon with the newborn
child, in Revelation 12 the child is exalted to heaven
and the woman carried to the desert for her own protection.

Some features of this international myth are also
found in the Roman imperial cult. A coin of Pergamum, e.g., shows the goddess Roma with the emperor. Roma, the Queen of Heaven, was worshiped as
the mother of the gods in the cities of Asia Minor and
her oldest temple stood in Smyrna, whereas her imperial child was celebrated as the "world's saviour" and
the sun-god Apollo. Such an allusion to the imperial
cult and the goddess Roma is probably intended here,
since the woman clothed with the sun clearly is the
anti-image of Babylon, the symbol of Rome and its allies in chapters 17–18.

The international ancient myth is, however, reinterpreted by John in terms of Jewish expectations. The stress on the travail of the woman is not derived from the myth but inspired by the Old Testament image of Israel-Sion in the messianic times. With the symbolic language of the ancient pagan myth, John thus evokes the image of the messianic child being born in the birthpangs of the messianic woes. In Revelation this child is without question Jesus Christ who is exalted and receives the powers of the messianic king (cf. Ps 2:9; Rv 11:18; 19:15). The "birth of the Messiah" is here therefore not the historical birth of Jesus but his exaltation and enthronement as the "firstborn of the dead" and the beginning of the new creation.

The figure of the dragon, serpent, crocodile, or sea monster also is familiar from ancient mythology and the Old Testament. In Old Testament-Jewish writings it frequently serves as a symbol of an oppressor nation like Egypt (Ps 74:14) and its ruler Pharaoh (Ez 32:3 ff), or as Syria and Babylon (cf. Is 27:1). In Daniel it is the symbol of the last great antidivine nation and the ruler opposing Israel (7:1–7). In this symbol-context, the red dragon is immediately understood as the ultimate foe of the people of God.

The woman, whose fate is announced in 12:6 and expanded on in the last section, has received very different interpretations. She is identified as the Israel of the Old Testament, or the New Testament, as the heavenly church or as the historical mother of Jesus, Mary. However, it is obvious that the vision is a mythological symbolization of transpersonal divine realities. If we observe how the figure of the "woman" functions in the symbol system of Revelation, then we recognize that the symbol is used either for the great harlot, Babylon/Rome, or for the New Jersualem coming down from heaven likened to a bride adorned for her husband (cf. 19:7ff; 21:2,9ff). As an eschatological reality it symbolizes not only the eschatologically saved people of God but also the renewed world. Thus the images of 12:6,13–18, like those of the sealing of the 144,000 and the measuring of the priestly worshipers, promise that the Christians will be eschatologically protected and saved, although the war waged with the beast might harm and kill them.

The central section, Revelation 12:7–12, reveals the deepest cause of the persecution and oppression experienced by the Christians at the time of John. The mythological symbolization of the "war in heaven" serves to explain in the Jewish language of myth that Satan or the Devil, the accuser and prosecutor of the Christians, has for a short time received the opportunity to exercise his power on earth after he was thrown out of heaven at the exaltation of Christ. The image of war is intertwined with that of a court trial in heaven, where Satan functioned as prosecutor and Michael as the defender of God's people.

The victory hymn of 12:10–12 announces the salvation, power, and kingdom of God and Christ. At the same time it asserts that the witnesses have won the victory because they have honored their redemption through Christ and not surrendered even in the face of death. Therefore, great rejoicing and feasting take place in the heavenly world while the third woe is announced to the earth and its inhabitants, over whom Satan exercises his oppressive power.

STUDY QUESTIONS: What is your understanding of myth? Why did John use the language of myth for communicating his prophetic revelation?

Revelation 12:18–14:5
THE CULT OF THE BEAST
AND THE FOLLOWERS
OF THE LAMB

The composition of this section has again the form of an inclusion: The mythical beast rising from the sea (13:1–10[a]) is followed by the "other" beast arising from the land (13:11–18[b]) which in turn is replaced by the Lamb standing on Mount Sion (14:1–5) whose mirror image is the first wild beast from the sea (a'). All three visionary images conclude with an explicit prophetic interpretation in the form of a warning (13:10), an apocalyptic parable (13:18), and a theological identification of the Lamb's followers.

The language of mythical symbolization is derived from the primeval myth of the two monsters who were separated and has many direct allusions to Daniel. Of the two monsters, Leviathan was to live in the abyss of the ocean, whereas Behemoth was to dwell on the dry land. According to Jewish folklore, these two primeval monsters will have messianic eschatological functions (cf. Ba 29:4,8; Ezr 6:49 ff). The Danielic patterns and overtones of the chapter point to a political interpretation of the monsters, especially since such a political interpretation of the Danielic four beasts was well established in Jewish literature of the time.

The statement of 12:18 is a transitional statement that interlinks the conclusion of 12:17 with the new image of the wild beast from the sea (13:1). It therefore is best understood as an introduction to the whole section, which begins with the images of the dragon standing at the shore of the sea and concludes with the image of the Lamb standing on Mount Sion. The whole section therefore develops the announcement of 12:17 that the dragon wages war with the rest of the woman's offspring who clearly are characterized as Christians. The rage of Satan against the woman as the symbol of the New Creation fuels the rage of the nations (11:18) who destroy the earth. Yet it is important to keep in mind that John also stresses again and again that the cruel war of the antidivine powers does not prove the powerlessness of God and Christ, nor does it express the positive will of God. The apocalyptic expression "it was given" emphasizes again and again that God permits and tolerates this life-destroying war but only for a very short time.

Revelation 13:1–10
THE PROPHETIC UNMASKING
OF ROMAN IMPERIAL POWER

$^{18}_{1}$ I was standing on the seashore. **13** Then I saw a beast emerge from the sea: it had seven heads and ten horns, with a coronet on each of its ten horns, and its heads were marked with blas-
2 phemous titles. ·I saw that the beast was like a leopard, with paws like a bear and a mouth like a lion; the dragon had handed over to it his own power and his throne and his worldwide authority.
3 I saw that one of its heads seemed to have had a fatal wound but that this deadly injury had healed and, after that, the whole world had marveled and
4 followed the beast. ·They prostrated themselves in front of the dragon because he had given the beast his authority; and they prostrated themselves in front of the beast, saying, "Who can compare with the beast? How could anybody de-
5 feat him?" ·For forty-two months the beast was allowed to mouth its boasts and blasphemies and
6 to do whatever it wanted; ·and it mouthed its blasphemies against God, against his name, his heavenly Tent and all those who are sheltered there.
7 It was allowed to make war against the saints and conquer them, and given power over every race,
8 people, language and nation; ·and all people of the world will worship it, that is, everybody whose name has not been written down since the foundation of the world in the book of life of the sac-

9 rificial Lamb. ·If anyone has ears to hear, let him
10 listen: ·Captivity for those who are destined for
captivity; the sword for those who are to die by
the sword. This is why the saints must have constancy and faith.

✠

The first wild beast emerges from the sea, where the
dragon stands (the reading "I was standing . . ." is a
later variant manuscript reading). The seashore is that
of the Mediterranean Sea on whose opposite shore
Rome is geographically located. To people of the province Asia Minor, it might have appeared as if the proconsul emerged annually from the sea at his arrival in
Ephesus. In a similar fashion, according to the Jewish
Apocalypse of Ezra, the eagle symbolizing Rome is
coming from the sea (Ezr 11:1). However the "sea"
has not just geographical meaning but also mythological since, according to ancient beliefs, the sea is a symbol of chaos, evil, and demonic powers (cf. also 9:2;
11:7).

The monster has ten horns with ten diadems, seven
heads like the dragon, and one huge mouth uttering
blasphemies. Its bizarre description combines all the
features of the four beasts of Daniel 7. Since the four
beasts in Daniel 7 represent different kingdoms and political powers, it is stressed here that the beast em-
bodies all political powers of the time. However, its
power is not self-generated, but it received its throne
and sovereignty from Satan whose throne is found in
Pergamum (2:13).

However, the beast is not only the viceroy of Satan's power but also the parodic mirror image of the
Lamb. One of the beast's heads looks "as though

slaughtered to death." The same Greek expression is used to characterize the Lamb. The statement that this deadly wound was healed is interpreted in 13:14 as the beast's resurrection from death. As Christ shares the throne of his Father (3:21; ch. 5), so the monster shares that of Satan. The monster's blasphemous names parody the unknown name of Christ who is the Word of God (cf. 19:12). As Christ's royal/priestly community is elected from all nations so the beast's and Satan's worshipers come from all nations, tongues, and peoples. The whole world prostrates in adoration before Satan and the beast, acknowledging and praising them in the language of the Psalms: "Yahweh, who can compare with you?" (cf. Ps 35:10).

The activity of the beast is directed against God and the dwellings of God's power. Therefore, the monster characterized as anti-Christ cannot but wage war against the "saints" and win the victory over them. The time of persecution and suffering is the same time as that of the two witnesses (11:7) and the protection of the woman (12:6,10) or that of the true worshipers (11:2). All these different images prophetically illuminate in different ways the eschatological times of tribulation before the end. However, the multivalent imagery of Revelation's mythological symbolization is clearly focused and concretized politically. John does not speak in general about sufferings or demonic realities but prophetically identifies the oppression of the Christians and other peoples as the Roman usurpation of God's power. Therefore, he ends this vision of the bizarre monster symbolizing Roman imperial power with a call that has concluded all the seven messages to the churches: Pay attention! The loyal resistance and faithfulness of the Christians cannot but be expressed by going into captivity or being executed. A peaceful coexistence between the worshipers of Satan and of the monster and those advocating God's and Christ's power and sovereignty is not possible. The war of the monster is total.

Revelation 13:11–18
THE PROPHETIC UNMASKING
OF THE IMPERIAL CULT

11 Then I saw a second beast; it emerged from the ground; it had two horns like a lamb, but made a
12 noise like a dragon. ·This second beast was servant to the first beast, and extended its authority everywhere, making the world and all its people worship the first beast, which had had the fatal
13 wound and had been healed. ·And it worked great miracles, even to calling down fire from heaven
14 on to the earth while people watched. ·Through the miracles which it was allowed to do on behalf of the first beast, it was able to win over the people of the world and persuade them to put up a statue in honor of the beast that had been
15 wounded by the sword and still lived. ·It was allowed to breathe life into this statue, so that the statue of the beast was able to speak, and to have anyone who refused to worship the statue of the
16 beast put to death. ·He compelled everyone— small and great, rich and poor, slave and citizen— to be branded on the right hand or on the fore-
17 head, ·and made it illegal for anyone to buy or sell anything unless he had been branded with the name of the beast or with the number of its name.
18 There is need for shrewdness here: if anyone is clever enough he may interpret the number of the beast: it is the number of a man, the number 666.

✠

Whereas the author elaborates the appearance and bizarre characteristics of the first monster, only briefly does he point out that the second monster has horns like a lamb but speaks like a dragon. Not its whole appearance but only its horns—the symbols of power—are likened to that of a lamb, whereby in the present context the reference is clearly to *the* Lamb and *the* Dragon. The second beast, subsequently called the pseudoprophet (cf. 16:13; 19:20; 20:10), exercises the power of the Lamb while it preaches the message and speaks the language of the Dragon.

Therefore, John does not so much elaborate the appearance as he stresses the function of the second beast or the pseudoprophet who seeks to persuade the whole world to worship and to prostrate before Satan and his earthly agent, the Roman emperor. As the Lamb created the new royal/priestly community for God (5:9–10), so the pseudoprophet intends to make the whole world into a cultic community of Satan that worships the emperor as divine (13:12). He accomplishes this goal by working miracles, by making a cultic image of the first monster, and finally by brandishing its followers with a mark on their foreheads or right hands.

First: Like Elijah the pseudoprophet works miracles in order to legitimize his activity. The second figure is thus the antifigure of the two prophetic witnesses who also act in the authority and power of Elijah. The visions of the two monsters from the sea and earth therefore seem to announce in mythological symbolization what was predicted in Mark 13:22, that false Christs and false prophets will arise and show signs and wonders. . . . However, Revelation reinterprets this traditional Christian endtime expectation in political terms.

Second: The pseudoprophet acts as the cultic-propagandistic agent by making an imperial image or statue that could speak. It was commonplace in antiquity that cultic images or statues could talk, even move, and that the priests of various cults could animate the images of their idols. However, the imperial image has not just a miraculous effect but it serves to identify publicly the true worshipers of the beast. As all were threatened with death who did not worship the image of Nebuchadnezzar (Dn 3:5-7), so here all those who do not worship the imperial image risk persecution and death (13:15). This feature points again to the imperial cult, since the citizens of the empire and especially the provinces expressed their loyalty toward Rome and the emperor by prostrating before an imperial cultic statue and burning incense in honor of the divine emperor. Finally, the name pseudoprophet for the second beast, as well as the reference to the imperial idols, refers us back to the opposing Christian prophets in the seven messages who might have argued with Paul that idols are "nothing" and that Christians are free to participate in the imperial cult. John in turn stresses that behind this cult stands Satan himself.

Third: The mark on their foreheads and right hands (cf. also 14:9,11; 16:2; 19:20; 20:4) is an antidote to the sealing of the Christians and characterizes the worshipers of the beast as the rival community to that of the Lamb. Moreover, the mark on the right hand clearly refers to the currency necessary for any economic transactions, since the coins of the Province had imprinted upon them the image of the emperor or the goddess Roma. This was the reason why the Jewish freedom fighters, the Zealots, did not use Roman coins and why Bar Kochba had minted his own Jewish currency. This economic impact of the beast's mark is underlined in 13:17.

The meaning of the number 666 must have been well known to Revelation's original audience but is no longer available to us. The solution had already been lost to Irenaeus in the second century. The challenge to puzzle out this number refers to the notion that the letters of the alphabet had numbers as their equivalent and could therefore be transcribed in a numerical way (e.g., a=1; b=2). It was therefore easy to transcribe letters into numbers but almost impossible to reverse the procedure if the meaning was not known. The author stresses that the number is that of a human person. Scholars have therefore suggested that 666 is the numerical equivalent of Nero Caesar, an abbreviated form of the full title of Domitian, or the intensification of the number six that means incompleteness and evil. Whatever the exact meaning of the number, its economic value and impact are obvious. As the vision of the first monster ended with the announcement of captivity and execution, so this vision ends with the threat of economic boycott of all those who do not participate in the prostration before the beast. The great tribulation of the endtime is thus reinterpreted here in political-economic terms. The economic and political oppression and persecution of the Christians and of all those who refuse to take part in the imperial cult have their deepest roots in the demonic anger of Satan which, in turn, fuels that of those who destroy the earth.

STUDY QUESTIONS: Who are the "destroyers of the earth" today? Why is the "flag" such a potent symbol today? What does this symbol have to do with being a Christian?

Revelation 14:1–5
THE ALTERNATIVE COMMUNITY

1 **14** Next in my vision I saw Mount Zion, and standing on it a Lamb who had with him a hundred and forty-four thousand people, all with his name and his Father's name written on their **2** foreheads. ·I heard a sound coming out of the sky like the sound of the ocean or the roar of thunder; it seemed to be the sound of harpists playing their **3** harps. ·There in front of the throne they were singing a new hymn in the presence of the four animals and the elders, a hymn that could only be learned by the hundred and forty-four thousand **4** who had been redeemed from the world. ·These are the ones who have kept their virginity and not been defiled with women; they follow the Lamb wherever he goes; they have been redeemed from amongst men to be the first-fruits for God and **5** for the Lamb. ·They never allowed a lie to pass their lips and no fault can be found in them.

✠

This section consists of a vision and audition (verses 1–3) followed by an explicit interpretation (verses 4–5). The vision pictures the alternative community of the Lamb, whereas the audition recalls the "new song" of 5:8–10.

The number 144,000 as well as the seal on their foreheads indicate that the followers of the Lamb are identical with those sealed in 7:1–8. Their location is not the historical Mount Sion nor the heavenly Sion, since 14:2 clearly distinguishes Sion from heaven, but the eschatological place of protection and liberation. According to Isaiah 24:23 and 25:7–10, at the end of time God will be proclaimed king on Mount Sion, death will be destroyed, and God's people will be liberated from their oppression and the slander against them. The prophet Joel stresses again and again that, on the Day of the Lord, Mount Sion will be the place of salvation for all those who call on the name of God. According to contemporary apocalypses, the Messiah will appear on Mount Sion with the elect, while the nations gather for eschatological war. He will punish the nations, kill the king of the last empire, and gather the community of the elect (Ezr 13:25–50; syr Bar 40:1 f; cf. also Rv 17:4). Thus the vision of the Lamb on Mount Sion clearly is the first in the series of the following judgment visions and announcements. At the same time it is also the counter-image to the vision of the first monster. This is underlined by the characterization and the interpretation of the 144,000.

The vision and audition describe the 144,000 in a threefold way. First, they have God's and the Lamb's names on their foreheads which characterizes them as the anti-image of the beast's worshipers. Like the Jewish high priest and the provincial high priest of the imperial cult, they have the name of God on their foreheads. Second, they alone are capable of learning the "new song" of the heavenly liturgy which was already mentioned in 5:8 ff. But whereas 5:8–10 elaborates the content of the "new song," 14:3 focuses on those who can learn it. It is significant that 14:3 stresses that they are redeemed from "the earth," which now suffers the eschatological wrath of God. Thus the vision and audition of 14:1-3 announce the same eschatological protection of the redeemed faithful that was promised in 7:1-8 and 11:1-2.

The interpretation of the vision centers not on the Lamb or on Mount Sion but on the identity of the 144,000. They are, as the first fruits of the harvest, the perfect offering and gift for God. They are the true followers of Christ because they refuse to participate in "the lie" and deception of the beast. Very difficult is their first characterization "they have not soiled themselves with women." A literal ascetic interpretation is unlikely since such a misogynist stance is nowhere else found in the New Testament. Moreover, celibacy is not stressed elsewhere in Revelation. Therefore, it is more likely that the phrase refers to idolatry and the imperial cult, since Babylon is seen as "the mother of all prostitutes" (17:5), "with whom all the kings of the earth have committed fornication" (17:8). The true followers of the Lamb have not drunk "from the wine of her fornication." They are members of the bride community of the Lamb.

In conclusion: 14:1-5 has a twofold function within the overall composition of Revelation. It pictures the alternative community of the Lamb living in the midst of the worshipers of the beast. At the same time it initiates the following series of eschatological judgment visions that, like the Synoptic-apocalyptic predictions, picture the last judgment in terms of a world harvest. The true followers of the Lamb are like the faultless first-fruit offerings of the earth. They are also the

promise that not all humanity will follow those who
"destroy the earth."

STUDY QUESTIONS: Who are the true followers of
Christ? Does their protection in the
endtime mean that they will be res-
cued from difficulties and suffering?

Revelation 14:6–13
THE ANNOUNCEMENT
OF JUDGMENT

The triple announcement of 14:6–13 already introduces the following visions of the bowl judgments that climax in the judgment of Babylon. At the same time it refers back to the alternative between the worship of the beast and the loyalty to God and the Lamb elaborated in chapters 12–13. The announcement of judgment is introduced and concluded by words of salvation.

6 Then I saw another angel, flying high overhead, sent to announce the Good News of eternity to all who live on the earth, every nation, race, language and tribe. ·He was calling, "Fear God and praise him, because the time has come for him to sit in judgment; worship the maker of heaven and earth and sea and every water-spring."

8 A second angel followed him, calling, "Babylon has fallen, Babylon the Great has fallen, Babylon which gave the whole world the wine of God's anger to drink."

9 A third angel followed, shouting aloud, "All those who worship the beast and his statue, or have had themselves branded on the hand or fore-

10 head, ·will be made to drink the wine of God's
fury which is ready, undiluted, in his cup of anger; in fire and brimstone they will be tortured in
the presence of the holy angels and the Lamb
11 and the smoke of their torture will go up for ever
and ever. There will be no respite, night or day,
for those who worshiped the beast or its statue or
12 accepted branding with its name." ·This is why
there must be constancy in the saints who keep
the commandments of God and faith in Jesus.
13 Then I heard a voice from heaven say to me,
"Write down: Happy are those who die in the
Lord! Happy indeed, the Spirit says; now they
can rest for ever after their work, since their good
deeds go with them."

☩

The angel flying in midheaven refers us back to the
eagle of 8:13 who announced the three woes. As coun-
terparts of the woes the message of the three angels is
"good news." The first angel calls all humanity to conversion in the words of early Christian missionary
preachers (cf. 1 Th 1:9 f; Ac 14:15 ff; 17:24 ff).
Moreover, according to the Synoptic apocalypse, the
Gospel had to be preached to all the nations before the
end would come (Mk 13:10; Mt 24:14). This expectation is shared by Revelation. The Gospel message of
the book is the call to worship the Creator, the living
God. Everyone receives the possibility of acknowledging the ultimate source of all life.

The second angel announces in traditional prophetic
words (cf. Is 24:9; Jr 51:7 f; Dn 4:27) that judgment
is executed over Babylon/Rome. This is a clear indica-
tion that the narrative of Revelation does not follow a
temporal sequence since the fall of Babylon/Rome will
only be narrated in chapters 17–18. The proclamation

of the third angel is considerably expanded. The punishment of the beast's worshipers is not an accurate description nor a literal prediction of their fate but a prophetic threat and exhortation expressed in metaphorical language. The function of this prophetic announcement is not an invitation for the Christians to gloat over the torture of their enemies but a call for steadfast resistance and loyal endurance. In A.D. 112 the emperor Trajan wrote to Pliny, the governor of Bithynia (a province in Asia Minor), that the Christians should be punished only if they are accused and convicted: Those who deny "that they are Christians, and make the fact plain by their actions, that is, by worshiping our Gods, shall obtain pardon." The threat of eternal punishment is a warning to Christians and non-Christians alike not to worship idols and not to participate in the imperial cult.

The message of the three angels is concluded with a beatitude that is pronounced by a "voice from heaven" and underlined by the command "write down." As Paul assures his communities that the dead "in Christ" will share in the resurrection (1 Th 4:16; 1 Co 15:17 f), so Revelation assures us that the Christians who have died can rest in peace because their lifework will vouch for them in the last judgment (cf. 20:12 f). The life-praxis of the Christians who have died is not forgotten.

STUDY QUESTION: The basic conversion in Revelation is the conversion to the Creator-God. How are we to live this conversion today?

Revelation 14:14–20
THE ESCHATOLOGICAL
HARVEST

The harvest theme links this vision with 14:1–5 that characterized the followers of the Lamb as the "first fruits," an offering without blemish. It also corresponds to the expectations of the Synoptic apocalypse (Mk 13:27; Mt 24:30) and the parables of the kingdom (cf. Mk 4:29; Mt 13:39). Revelation expands this eschatological expectation insofar as it follows the pattern of Joel 4:13 by paralleling the harvest image with that of the vintage. Although some scholars suggest that both images have the same meaning, it is more likely that the harvest of the grain is a positive image whereas that of the grapes speaks of the wrath of God.

14 Now in my vision I saw a white cloud and, sitting on it, one like a son of man with a gold crown
15 on his head and a sharp sickle in his hand. ·Then another angel came out of the sanctuary, and shouted aloud to the one sitting on the cloud, "Put your sickle in and reap: harvest time has come
16 and the harvest of the earth is ripe." ·Then the one sitting on the cloud set his sickle to work on the earth, and the earth's harvest was reaped.
17 Another angel, who also carried a sharp sickle,

18 came out of the temple in heaven, ·and the angel
   in charge of the fire left the altar and shouted
   aloud to the one with the sharp sickle, "Put your
   sickle in and cut all the bunches off the vine of the
19 earth; all its grapes are ripe." ·So the angel set his
   sickle to work on the earth and harvested the
   whole vintage of the earth and put it into a huge
20 winepress, the winepress of God's anger, ·outside
   the city, where it was trodden until the blood that
   came out of the winepress was up to the horses'
   bridles as far away as sixteen hundred furlongs.

☩

The image of the one in human form sitting on a
white cloud alludes to Daniel 7:13 but clearly identifies
the figure with the Parousia Christ in 1:7 and 19:11.
He is the center of chapter 14 insofar as he is preceded
and followed by three angels. According to traditional
Christian expectation, at the Day of God Christ will
send out angels to gather the elect from the ends of the
earth (Mk 13:27). However, the harvest here does not
just mean the ingathering of the elect but of all those
who accept "the eternal Gospel" since 14:1–3 has already imaged the gathering of the elect by Christ.

More difficult to understand is the image of the vintage. It is argued that it has the same positive meaning
as the harvest because the vine was a traditional symbol for Israel and the church and "outside the city was
the proper place for the martyrdom of those who held
the testimony of Jesus" (Caird). However, the image of
the "winepress of the wrath of God" points to 19:15
where it is clearly stated that Christ will tread the winepress of the fury of the wrath of God, the Almighty.
The vintage image thus seems to be influenced by

Isaiah 63:3–6, the picture of Yahweh's terrible vengeance.

STUDY QUESTIONS: What function do the language and images of judgment have in Revelation? Are they to evoke guilt and fear or loyalty and strength?

Revelation 15:1
THE THIRD PORTENT
IN THE SKY

Revelation 15:1 is clearly the introduction to the following vision of the seven bowls or goblets. This introduction characterizes them as antipode to the first great portent in the sky, the woman in cosmic splendor, because the whole series climaxes in the seventh bowl, the destruction of Babylon, which is greatly elaborated in chapters 17–18.

¹ **15** What I saw next, in heaven, was a great and wonderful sign: seven angels were bringing the seven plagues that are the last of all, because they exhaust the anger of God.

✠

Revelation 15:2–4
THE ESCHATOLOGICAL PRAISE
OF GOD'S JUSTICE

The praise of the eschatological victors serves as a climax to the visions of the small scroll 10:1–14:20 and, at the same time, as an interlude to the bowl visions that prophetically interpret the narration of God's wrath. The theological motifs of Israel's Exodus as the liberation from the oppressive power of Egypt, which like a red thread was woven into the preceding vision, are here focused and explicitly determine the following plague visions.

2 I seemed to see a glass lake suffused with fire, and standing by the lake of glass, those who had fought against the beast and won, and against his statue and the number which is his name. They all had
3 harps from God, ·and they were singing the hymn of Moses, the servant of God, and of the Lamb:

"How great and wonderful are all your works,
Lord God Almighty;
just and true are all your ways,
King of nations.
4 Who would not revere and praise your name,
O Lord?

You alone are holy,
and all the pagans will come and adore you
for the many acts of justice you have shown."

✠

In this climactic vision of the little prophetic scroll,
John has tied together the images and symbols of the
previous vision into an impressive vision of hope. The
"lake of glass" refers back to 4:6, the "fire" to the
wrath of God (cf. 8:5), the "harps" remind us of the
"new song" of 5:8 and 14:2, the characterization of
the persons as "victors" is a fulfillment of the promises
to the victors at the end of the seven messages, the
"lake of glass" reminds us of the Exodus-plagues of
the previous seven cycles, and the victory in the war
against the beast ties the vision to the preceding chapters. As the Israelites after crossing the Red Sea sang
the victory song of liberation (Ex 15:1 ff), so here the
conquerors sing a hymn of deliverance in praise of
God's justice.

Almost every word of this hymn can be traced to the
Old Testament (Dt 32:4; Ps 86:8 ff; 111:2; Am 4:13;
Ml 1:11; Ps 11:2; 139:14). The most influential text
is, however, Exodus 15:1–8. The "Song of Moses" has
become the "Song of the Lamb" (the new song), insofar as both praise God's redemptive activity in the deliverance and liberation of the people of God. However, the hymn is also a positive response to the
"eternal Gospel" because it announces that the justice
of God, who is like Caesar the king of the nations, will
move the nations of the earth to come and worship
God. Revelation announces liberation and salvation
not only for the Christian community, but for all the

nations who are now oppressed and long to experience the justice of God.

STUDY QUESTIONS: Why is this vision so important for the theological understanding of Revelation? Can one understand the basic Gospel message of the book if one neglects or denies its universal hope for liberation and justice?

C'. The Trial and Sentencing of Babylon/Rome
Revelation 15:5 to 19:10

INTRODUCTION

As we have seen, this section is introduced by the angelic announcements in 14:6–13 and initiated by the presentation of the bowl angels in 15:1 and the interlude of deliverance in 15:2–4. However, it is difficult to decide where the section ends, since the Babylon visions are formally clearly marked as a part of the last bowl vision and at the same time serve as the first part of the inclusion 17:1–19:10(a), 19:11–21:8(b), and 21:9–22:10(a'). Here again we have to remember that John does not think in terms of sections or divisions but intends to interlace and join different parts of the composition with each other. The Babylon visions are thus a "joint" that interconnects the two vision series of eschatological judgment with each other and at the same time point to the climax of the vision series of judgment in the vision of the New Jerusalem.

Revelation 15:5–16
THE SEVEN BOWLS
OF GOD'S WRATH

The seven bowl series of judgments parallels and
intensifies the symbolization of the trumpet series.
Whereas the trumpet plagues destroyed only one third
of the earth, the bowl plagues have a total effect. The
reaction of people to the bowl plagues is similar to that
evoked by the trumpet plagues. The repeated emphasis
that people did not repent reflects the Egyptian-plague
pattern according to which Pharaoh and his people did
not repent. In addition, the reaction to the plagues of
the bowls reveal the true allegiance of people who, like
the beast, blaspheme the living God. Finally, the bowl
sequence follows the trumpet pattern in that the first
four plagues are visited upon the earth, sea, inland
waters, and the heavenly bodies, whereas the last three
afflict the demonic powers of the underworld. However, while the effects of the four trumpets prove only
to be incidental to people, the bowl punishments are
clearly directed toward the antidivine community of the
beast worshipers. Although this indicates that the bowl
series materially functions differently than the trumpet
series, it also shows that both plague series have formally the same function. They do not speak of different
eschatological events but recapitulate each other and

symbolically illuminate different dimensions of the Great Day of the Lord.

⁵ After this, in my vision, the sanctuary, the Tent ⁶ of the Testimony, opened in heaven, ·and out came the seven angels with the seven plagues, wearing pure white linen, fastened round their ⁷ waists with golden girdles. ·One of the four animals gave the seven angels seven golden bowls filled with the anger of God who lives for ever and ⁸ ever. ·The smoke from the glory and the power of God filled the temple so that no one could go into it until the seven plagues of the seven angels were completed.

¹ **16** Then I heard a voice from the sanctuary shouting to the seven angels, "Go, and empty the seven bowls of God's anger over the earth."

² The first angel went and emptied his bowl over the earth; at once, on all the people who had been branded with the mark of the beast and had worshiped its statue, there came disgusting and virulent sores.

³ The second angel emptied his bowl over the sea, and it turned to blood, like the blood of a corpse, and every living creature in the sea died.

⁴ The third angel emptied his bowl into the rivers and water-springs and they turned into blood. ⁵ Then I heard the angel of water say, "You are the holy He-Is-and-He-Was, the Just One, and this ⁶ is a just punishment: ·they spilt the blood of the saints and the prophets, and blood is what you have given them to drink; it is what they deserve." ⁷ And I heard the altar itself say, "Truly, Lord God Almighty, the punishments you give are true and just."

⁸ The fourth angel emptied his bowl over the sun and it was made to scorch people with its ⁹ flames; ·but though people were scorched by the

fierce heat of it, they cursed the name of God who had the power to cause such plagues, and they would not repent and praise him.

10 The fifth angel emptied his bowl over the throne of the beast and its whole empire was plunged into darkness. Men were biting their 11 tongues for pain, ·but instead of repenting for what they had done, they cursed the God of heaven because of their pains and sores.

12 The sixth angel emptied his bowl over the great river Euphrates; all the water dried up so that a way was made for the kings of the East to come 13 in. ·Then from the jaws of dragon and beast and false prophet I saw three foul spirits come; they 14 looked like frogs ·and in fact were demon spirits, able to work miracles, going out to all the kings of the world to call them together for the war of 15 the Great Day of God the Almighty.—·This is how it will be: I shall come like a thief. Happy is the man who has stayed awake and not taken off his clothes so that he does not go out naked and ex- 16 pose his shame.—·They called the kings together at the place called, in Hebrew, Armageddon.

17 The seventh angel emptied his bowl into the air, and a voice shouted from the sanctuary, "The 18 end has come." ·Then there were flashes of light- ning and peals of thunder and the most violent earthquake that anyone has ever seen since there 19 have been men on the earth. ·The Great City was split into three parts and the cities of the world collapsed; Babylon the Great was not forgotten: God made her drink the full winecup of his anger. 20 Every island vanished and the mountains disap- 21 peared; ·and hail, with great hailstones weighing a talent each, fell from the sky on the people. They cursed God for sending a plague of hail; it was the most terrible plague.

☩

Like the trumpet series, so do the bowl plagues
come forth from the heavenly temple. The open "tent
of the Testimony" refers to Israel's sojourn in the wil-
derness and recalls the climax of the trumpet plagues
in 11:19. The introduction in 15:1 is restated and
elaborated insofar as the seven angels are pictured in
the vestments of the high priest, and the seven plagues
are symbolized in the image of golden bowls. The symbol of the "golden bowl" alludes to the golden bowls
of incense in 5:8 which is identified with the prayers of
the saints. The smoke filling the temple and the sounds
of theophany recall the smoke of incense symbolizing
the prayers of the saints in the introductory vision to
the seven trumpets (8:2-5). Fueled by the fire from
the altar, it exploded in the terrible sounds of theophany. Thus the seven golden bowls filled with the
wrath of God announce in symbolic language the same
early Christian conviction expressed in 2 Thessalonians
1:6: "God will very rightly repay with injury those
who are injuring you . . ." The bowl plagues are an
answer to the prayer and outcry of the Christians for
justice. They are also a warning to Christians and non-
Christians alike not to become members of the im-
perial-cult community.

The followers of the beast and its universal community are the object of God's wrath. This is clearly stated
in the execution of the first bowl, in the destruction of
Babylon/Rome in the climactic seventh bowl, and in
the concentration of the fifth-bowl plague on the
throne of the beast. The bowl plagues do not bring
about repentance as those of the two prophetic
witnesses did (11:13) but make public the true followers of the beast who blaspheme God.

The sixth and the seventh bowls announce the destruction of Babylon/Rome which will be more fully

developed in chapters 17–18. The sixth bowl shows the
advance of the enemy kings of the East (verse 12) who
will lay siege to Rome (17:15–18), whereas the seventh bowl confirms the fall of Babylon announced
in 14:8 and lamented in chapter 18. Revelation
16:13–16 is not a part of the sixth bowl since the
kings from the East must be distinguished from the
kings of the earth assembled for the great battle on the
last day. Therefore, 16:13–16 must be understood as
an interlude that is the *formal* equivalent of the interludes before the seventh seal (ch. 7) and the seventh
trumpet (chs. 10–11).

The three evil spirits looking like frogs are the func-
tionaries of the demonic trinity, the dragon, beast, and
pseudoprophet. They assemble their army for the final
battle at a mythological place called in Hebrew Har-
Magedon or Mount of Megiddo. Like that of the number 666, the intended meaning of this name eludes all
scholarly attempts of definition. Yet it is important to
keep in mind that the author's mythological-symbolic
language is multivalent and should not be reduced to a
one-dimensional definition. John is not interested in
giving geographic-eschatological information but prophetic interpretation. He announces here the great eschatological battle that will be more fully developed in
19:11–20:10. At the same time the interjection of a
traditional Christian prophetic warning in verse 15 indicates how this mythological symbolization of the Day
of the Lord should be understood. The impressive images and mythological narration of the eschatological
endtime and judgment should not lead to speculation
and calculation. Christ will come like a thief in the
night (cf. 1 Th 5:2 ff; Mt 24:42 ff; 2 P 3:10; also
Rv 3:3). One should always be prepared.

However, the mythological symbolization of the eschatological wrath of God does not just serve prophetic exhortation but it also gives prophetic assurance and encouragement. Deviating from the plagues pattern of the trumpets, John inserts after the third bowl plague a twofold acclamation that theologically interprets the whole plague series. The angel of the waters and the altar in 16:4-7 (cf. 6:9; 8:3-5; 9:13; 14:18) praises God's justice and faithful execution of judgment, echoing the song of Moses and the Lamb in 15:2-4. God's justice will prevail. It is, however, neither inflicted from the outside nor with despotic arbitrariness. Justice is not an alien imposition by some external authority. Instead justice is the conviction that each act brings about consequences that must be faced responsibly. It is God who has the power to see to it that all people have to bear the consequences of their actions. All receive what is their due. The Greek text does not speak of punishments but about judgment and justice. Not punitive torments but equity and vindication are the motive and goal of God's wrath and judgment.

STUDY QUESTIONS: Why is it important to distinguish between punishment and execution of justice? Why is Revelation more concerned about justice than about love?

Revelation 17:1–19:10
THE EXECUTION
OF BABYLON FOR MURDER

This section could be compared to a triptych with three panels. After a general introductory headline in 17:1–2, the world capital, Babylon, is described and interpreted in the first panel (17:3–18). The second panel (18:1–24) is stylistically quite different insofar as the destruction of the great city is not described but only reflected in the dirges of the kings, merchants, and shipowners. The legal claim of the persecuted Christians against Rome is now granted. The powerful capital of the world is destroyed not just because it has persecuted the church but also because it has unlawfully killed many other persons. Revelation 18:24 must therefore be understood as the theological key to the whole Babylon series of judgments. The third panel presents the heavenly liturgy praising the justice of God's judgments and announcing the marriage feast of the Lamb (19:1–8). The whole is framed by the conclusion stressing that worship belongs only and solely to God (19:9–10).

The whole section is the fulfillment of the announcement of Babylon/Rome's judgment in 14:8 and a more elaborate close-up of the seventh bowl plague. At the same time, the figure of Babylon/Rome is the counterpoint image to the heavenly woman clothed with the sun in chapter 12 and the contrast image to the bride of the Lamb, the New Jerusalem. This is formally indicated insofar as the Babylon visions are the climax of the third great "portent in heaven" and introduced by the same bowl angel who shows John the New Jerusalem. John thus uses the image of a woman to symbolize the present murderous reality of Rome as well as the life-nurturing reality of the New World of God. However, it must not be overlooked that such female imagery was a given for John because then as today cities and countries are understood to be feminine. Moreover, centuries before Revelation, the Hebrew prophets had used the image of the bride, the wife, or the prostitute either for Jerusalem and Israel or for other nations and their capitals. Therefore, the imagery of Revelation would be totally misunderstood if it were seen as referring to the actual behavior of individual women. To the contrary, here more than in other sections Revelation relies for its imagery and language on the prophetic works of the Hebrew Bible. While, for example, the image of the Lamb or the two beasts refers to actual persons, the images of the heavenly woman, of the bride, or of the prostitute symbolize cities as the places of human culture and political organization.

Revelation 17:1–18
ROME AND ITS POWER

Like a headline, 17:1–2 summarizes the content of the whole triptych that portrays the sentence and judgment of Rome, the powerful capital of the world. It is characterized as an international city with the metaphor of the "many waters" (cf. verse 15). The label of the city as "the great prostitute" is probably derived from Isaiah 23:17 which especially in its Greek form understands the international commerce and wealth of Tyre as the "hire" paid to a prostitute. The metaphorical statement "the kings of the earth have committed fornication with her" means that Rome has usurped and perverted the political power of all its provinces. Therefore, its corruption and violence affect all the inhabitants of the world.

17 1 One of the seven angels that had the seven bowls came to speak to me, and said, "Come here and I will show you the punishment given to the famous prostitute who rules en- 2 throned beside abundant waters, ·the one with whom all the kings of the earth have committed fornication, and who has made all the population of the world drunk with the wine of her adultery." 3 He took me in spirit to a desert, and there I saw a

woman riding a scarlet beast which had seven heads and ten horns and had blasphemous titles
4 written all over it. ·The woman was dressed in purple and scarlet, and glittered with gold and jewels and pearls, and she was holding a gold winecup filled with the disgusting filth of her for-
5 nication; ·on her forehead was written a name, a cryptic name: "Babylon the Great, the mother of all the prostitutes and all the filthy practices on the
6 earth." ·I saw that she was drunk, drunk with the blood of the saints, and the blood of the martyrs of Jesus; and when I saw her, I was completely
7 mystified. ·The angel said to me, "Don't you understand? Now I will tell you the meaning of this woman, and of the beast she is riding, with the seven heads and the ten horns.

8   "The beast you have seen once was and now is not; he is yet to come up from the Abyss, but only to go to his destruction. And the people of the world, whose names have not been written since the beginning of the world in the book of life, will think it miraculous when they see how the beast once was and now is not and is still to come.
9 Here there is need for cleverness, for a shrewd mind; the seven heads are the seven hills, and the woman is sitting on them.

10   "The seven heads are also seven emperors. Five of them have already gone, one is here now, and one is yet to come; once here, he must stay for a
11 short while. ·The beast, who once was and now is not, is at the same time the eighth and one of the seven, and he is going to his destruction.

12   "The ten horns are ten kings who have not yet been given their royal power but will have royal authority only for a single hour and in association
13 with the beast. ·They are all of one mind in putting their strength and their powers at the beast's dis-
14 posal, ·and they will go to war against the Lamb; but the Lamb is the Lord of lords and the King of kings, and he will defeat them and they will be defeated by his followers, the called, the chosen, the faithful."

15 The angel continued, "The waters you saw, beside which the prostitute was sitting, are all the peoples, the populations, the nations and the languages. ·But the time will come when the ten
16 horns and the beast will turn against the prostitute, and strip off her clothes and leave her naked; then they will eat her flesh and burn the remains
17 in the fire. ·In fact, God influenced their minds to do what he intended, to agree together to put their royal powers at the beast's disposal until the
18 time when God's words should be fulfilled. ·The woman you saw is the great city which has authority over all the rulers on earth."

☩

After a new introduction, John describes Babylon/Rome in its great splendor. However, the following interpretation first focuses on the beast before it sketches the desolation of Babylon and finally climaxes in the definition: It is the great city that has the ruling power over the kings of the earth. John is carried in prophetic inspiration to the desert, probably because he sees Babylon being made into a desert (verse 16) according to the decree of God.

Like a goddess, Babylon rides on the beast which has many blasphemous names written on it. The splendor and wealth of Babylon are dazzling even to John. As do the followers of the Lamb, so too does the image of Rome have a name written on its forehead which alludes to the great Mother Goddess. In her hands is a golden cup filled with idolatry and detestable things. At the same time the contents of the cup are identified with the blood of the Christians which has intoxicated the great city.

In 17:7–18 a lengthy explanation of the beast on

whom the woman rides is given. Like the number 666 in 13:18, this explanation has received much attention by exegetes since it seems to indicate the time when the author is writing. The seven heads of the beast are said to be the seven hills on which the woman sits. Thus the great city Babylon is clearly identified with Rome. The hills in turn are identified with seven kings, of whom: five have fallen, one exists, and another is still to come (although, when he comes, he will remain only a little while). The beast in turn is the eighth, although it belongs to the seven. Two possible approaches to the riddle are suggested. One interpretation suggests that this explanation should be understood as symbolic and not allegoric. The seven emperors are a symbolic seven and not actual emperors. As at the sixth bowl and the sixth trumpet, the demonic forces develop the greatest power; so John places himself at the time of the sixth emperor to let his readers know that they live at the height of the destructive imperial power but that the judgment of this power is imminent. As the beast usurps the divine attributes of God (17:8), so it assumes the number six as the antichristic eight because the number of Jesus was 888 (The numerical equivalent of the name *Iesous* in Greek is: I=10; e=8; s=200; o=70; u=400; s=200).

The second attempt to solve the riddle is more likely but also not conclusive. This second approach insists that the seven heads are actual Roman emperors. Yet no agreement exists as to who should be counted as the first emperor of the series. Since the author, however, must have known that a seventh will come, the most probable solution is that he is Trajan who was designated emperor shortly before Nerva's death who then, in turn, must have been the sixth of the series. Revelation would thus be written in 97/98 shortly after the murder of Domitian. The Greek word for "they have fallen" speaks of the preceding emperors who have suffered violent deaths, namely Caesar, Caligula, Nero, and Domitian. This suggestion comes close to the traditional date of Revelation which according to Ireneus was written toward the end of the reign of Domitian (81–96).

The statement that the beast was one of the seven alludes to the legend that Nero would return or be resurrected. With the help of the Parthians he would avenge himself and destroy Rome. This expectation seems to be reflected in the ten kings who will give their power to the beast and destroy the great city. They are, therefore, not identical with the kings of the earth, who have given their power to Babylon. They seem to be identical with the demonic army called together by the three demonic frogs and identical with "Gog and Magog" in 20:7 ff. They will make war with the messianic king whose followers are presented in 14:1–5 and 20:4–6, but the Lamb will overcome them (cf. 19:11 ff). The explanation given in 17:7–18 thus seems to underline that Babylon symbolizes the goddess Roma and the Roman empire.

Because of John's harsh indictment and criticism of Rome/Babylon, exegetes often attempt to diminish the political implications of John's vision because it appears to contradict other New Testament writings that have a more positive attitude to the Roman state (cf. Rm 13 or 1 P). However, Babylon the Great is not the symbol of the "archetypal enmity" against God or of the "decadence of all civilization." The vision also does not call for "an appreciation of the transience of life and the fleeting character of wealth and power" (Yarbro Collins). Rome in its splendor, being carried and supported by the beast, is the symbol of the imperial power and cult. As such, it is for John the powerful incarnation of international oppression and murder. Rome is intoxicated with the blood not only of the saints, but also of all those slaughtered on earth. Rome's power and wealth are enormous. Its power is expanded and its decrees carried out in the provinces that support Roman idolatry and persecution of the Christians.

Revelation 18:1–24
THE PROPHETIC PROCLAMATION
OF ROME'S JUDGMENT

The magnificent picture of Rome flaunting its wealth
and power shifts to a scene of doom. The vision of a
great angel in heavenly splendor and the announcement
of Babylon's fall (18:1–3) are followed by a double prophetic oracle (18:4–5,6–8). The series of
dirges and lamentation over Babylon (18:9–19) climaxes in a prophetic call of praise that at the same
time prepares for the concluding hymns in 19:1–8. The
whole chapter ends with a prophetic sign-action and a
prophetic summary of Rome's indictment: Its crime
was murder (18:21–23,24).

Chapter 18 is the middle panel within the overall
triptych of 17:1–19:10. At the same time, the chapter
is composed like a triptych within a triptych. Two
proclamations of judgment (18:1–8,21–24) frame the
series of dirges (18:9–19) which, in turn, is again
composed in a tripartite fashion. The central lament of
the merchants (18:11–16) is flanked by that of the
kings (18:9–10) and the shipowners (18:17–19). The
whole is an artful literary composition with imaginative
power. John achieves a powerful unitary composition,
although he derives his language and imagery almost
verbatim from Jewish sources. His artistic skill proves

itself in the interweaving of various, often contradictory, traditions into a unitary composition.

¹ **18** After this, I saw another angel come down from heaven, with great authority given to ² him; the earth was lit up with his glory. ·At the top of his voice he shouted, "Babylon has fallen, Babylon the Great has fallen, and has become the haunt of devils and a lodging for every foul spirit ³ and dirty, loathsome bird. ·All the nations have been intoxicated by the wine of her prostitution; every king in the earth has committed fornication with her, and every merchant grown rich through her debauchery."

⁴ A new voice spoke from heaven; I heard it say, "Come out, my people, away from her, so that you do not share in her crimes and have the same ⁵ plagues to bear. ·Her sins have reached up to ⁶ heaven, and God has her crimes in mind: ·she is to be paid in her own coin. She must be paid double the amount she exacted. She is to have a dou- ⁷ bly strong cup of her own mixture. ·Every one of her shows and orgies is to be matched by a torture or a grief. I am the queen on my throne, she says to herself, and I am no widow and shall never be ⁸ in mourning. ·For that, within a single day, the plagues will fall on her: disease and mourning and famine. She will be burned right up. The Lord God has condemned her, and he has great power."

⁹ There will be mourning and weeping for her by the kings of the earth who have fornicated with her and lived with her in luxury. They see the ¹⁰ smoke as she burns, ·while they keep at a safe distance from fear of her agony. They will say:

"Mourn, mourn for this great city,
Babylon, so powerful a city,
doomed as you are within a single hour."

¹¹ There will be weeping and distress over her

among all the traders of the earth when there is
12 nobody left to buy their cargoes of goods; ·their
stocks of gold and silver, jewels and pearls, linen
and purple and silks and scarlet; all the sandal-
wood, every piece in ivory or fine wood, in bronze
13 or iron or marble; ·the cinnamon and spices, the
myrrh and ointment and incense; wine, oil, flour
and corn; their stocks of cattle, sheep, horses and
chariots, their slaves, their human cargo.

14   "All the fruits you had set your hearts on have
failed you; gone for ever, never to return, is your
life of magnificence and ease."

15   The traders who had made a fortune out of her
will be standing at a safe distance from fear of
16 her agony, mourning and weeping. ·They will be
saying:

"Mourn, mourn for this great city;
for all the linen and purple and scarlet that you
  wore,
for all your finery of gold and jewels and pearls;
17 your riches are all destroyed within a single hour."

All the captains and seafaring men, sailors and all
those who make a living from the sea will be keep-
18 ing a safe distance, ·watching the smoke as she
burns, and crying out, "Has there ever been a city
19 as great as this!" ·They will throw dust on their
heads and say, with tears and groans:

"Mourn, mourn for this great city
  whose lavish living has made a fortune
  for every owner of a sea-going ship;
  ruined within a single hour.

20 "Now heaven, celebrate her downfall, and all you
saints, apostles and prophets: God has given judgment for you against her."

21   Then a powerful angel picked up a boulder like
a great millstone, and as he hurled it into the sea,
he said, "That is how the great city of Babylon is
going to be hurled down, never to be seen again.

22 "Never again in you, Babylon,

will be heard the song of harpists and minstrels,
the music of flute and trumpet;
never again will craftsmen of every skill be found
or the sound of the mill be heard;

23 never again will shine the light of the lamp,
never again will be heard
the voices of bridegroom and bride.
Your traders were the princes of the earth,
all the nations were under your spell.

24 In her you will find the blood of prophets and
saints, and all the blood that was ever shed on
earth."

✠

The central images and theological motifs of this
section are the splendor, wealth, and power of Rome,
and the justice of God's judgments. The whole scene is
conceived in terms of a universal courtroom, in which
a class-action suit takes place. The plaintiff classes are
the Christians and all those killed on earth (18:24),
the defendant is Babylon/Rome, the charge is murder
in the interest of power and idolatry, the judge is God.
As was previously announced in 14:8, Babylon/Rome
has lost this lawsuit and therefore its associates break
out in lamentation and mourning, while the heavenly
court and the Christians rejoice over the justice given
to them. The judge has acknowledged their legal complaints and claims to justice and has pronounced the
sentence against Rome which will be executed by the
beast and the ten horns as divine henchmen. Verse 20
should therefore be translated: God has exacted justice
from her on the basis of your legal claims. To misunderstand this legal mythologization as an expression of

Revelation's hate for civilization or as a sign of life's transience is a serious misunderstanding of Revelation's theology of justice.

The first temple of the goddess Roma was erected in Smyrna in 195 B.C.E., while Pergamum had become a center of the imperial cult in Asia Minor. It also became the religious and political center of the *Koinon,* the organization of the cities, of Asia. At the temple of Roma and Augustus in Pergamum, the Koinon assembled annually for the celebration of games in honor of Rome and Augustus. Although religious in character, the assembly of the Asian cities came to play an important political role in imperial administration. As the kings and cities of the Hellenistic world lost or gave their power to Rome, so they relinquished the honors and cults paid to them by the Greek and Asian cities either to the goddess Roma or to the Roman emperor. Therefore, Rome's political domination is supported and augmented by the idolatry of the nations.

The close economic ties between Rome and the provinces and the international commerce of the Roman world-state fostered the growth of economic wealth not only in Rome but also in the provinces. Historians of antiquity point out that never before had people known the same measure of stability and prosperity as in the Roman empire of the first century. However, only the provincial elite and the Italian immigrants, especially the shipowners and merchants, were reaping the wealth of the empire's prosperity, while the heavy burden of taxation impoverished the great majority of the provincial population. Thus a relatively small minority of the Asian cities benefited from the international commerce of the Roman empire, whereas the large masses of the city population lived in dire poverty or slavery (18:13). The author of Revelation is clearly on the side of the poor and oppressed, insofar as he sharply criticizes the community of Laodicea, which boasts of its riches, and insofar as he announces judgment and destruction for the rich and powerful of this earth (6:12–17; 17:4; 18:3,15–19,23). Economic oppression and retaliation are two of the beast's most powerful weapons for persuading people to participate in the imperial cult. Therefore, the two communities of Smyrna and Philadelphia, which have little power and are poor, receive no prophetic censure. Yet Revelation's theology is not so much interested in describing the "reversal of fate," because of an unchristian resentment of civilization or of the city, as it is in spelling out hope and encouragement for those who struggle for economic survival and freedom from persecution and murder.

The element of prophetic exhortation and hope is expressed in the twofold oracle in 18:4–8 and in the call for rejoicing in 18:20. While the oracle in 18:6–8 and the call to rejoicing in 18:20 pronounce the sentence on Babylon and confirm that God has seen to it that justice is done, the exhortation "come out of her, my people," alludes to the Exodus motif. As in the Old Testament, the exodus refers to Sodom, Egypt, and Babylon (cf. Jr 50:8; 51:6,45), so here the people of God are called to leave the great city that was in 11:8 called Sodom and Egypt. Since the great city Babylon represents the whole of the Roman empire, the call to "come out of her" must be understood metaphorically. It is a call not to cooperate in Babylon's injustice, idolatry, and murder. At the same time this call has a similar function as the sealing of the 144,000 in chapter 7 and as the measuring of the true worshipers in 11:1–2.

It announces the eschatological protection of those
who remained faithful at the Great Day of the Lord.

STUDY QUESTIONS: Why is the judgment motif so prev-
alent in Revelation 17–18? Do you
think exegetes understand Revelation when they interpret this motif
as "vengeance" or "hate for civilization" or "rejection of city life"?

Revelation 19:1–10
THE SALVATION
OF GOD'S REIGN

The whole section climaxes in a double audition. Its content and compositional functions are the same as those of 7:9–17; 11:15–19; 12:10–12; 15:2–4. It parallels and anticipates 21:1–22:5. While the antiphony of the heavenly choir proclaims God's justice and judgment (the major motifs of the preceding chapters), the second hymn rejoices because the marriage feast of the Lamb has come (the major motif of the following chapters). The whole section concludes with a beatitude or macarism and a dialogue between the angel and the seer. This dialogue is not only very similar in form and content to 19:9 f but also concludes section 21:9–22:9.

¹ **19** After this I seemed to hear the great sound of a huge crowd in heaven, singing, "Alleluia! Victory and glory and power to our God! ² He judges fairly, he punishes justly, and he has condemned the famous prostitute who corrupted the earth with her fornication; he has avenged his ³ servants that she killed." ·They sang again, "Alleluia! The smoke of her will go up for ever and

⁴ ever." ·Then the twenty-four elders and the four animals prostrated themselves and worshiped God seated there on his throne, and they cried, "Amen, Alleluia."

⁵ Then a voice came from the throne; it said, "Praise our God, you servants of his and all who,

⁶ great or small, revere him." ·And I seemed to hear the voices of a huge crowd, like the sound of the ocean or the great roar of thunder, answering, "Alleluia! The reign of the Lord our God Al-

⁷ mighty has begun; ·let us be glad and joyful and give praise to God, because this is the time for

⁸ the marriage of the Lamb. ·His bride is ready, and she has been able to dress herself in dazzling white linen, because her linen is made of the good

⁹ deeds of the saints." ·The angel said, "Write this: Happy are those who are invited to the wedding feast of the Lamb," and he added, "All the things you have written are true messages from God."

¹⁰ Then I knelt at his feet to worship him, but he said to me, "Don't do that: I am a servant just like you and all your brothers who are witnesses to Jesus. It is God that you must worship." The witness Jesus gave is the same as the spirit of prophecy.

✠

The three Hallelujahs of heaven and earth are the response to the call to praise in 18:20 and correspond to the three dirges over Babylon. The word Hallelujah is derived from the Hebrew words *halal* and *Yah* (Praise Yahweh) and alludes to the psalms of the Passover liturgy celebrating the Exodus from Egypt (Ps 113–18). Three choirs sing the antiphony of praise: the heavenly multitude (verses 1–3), the twenty-four elders, and four living creatures who are mentioned here for the last time in Revelation (verse

4), and the great multitude of people on earth (verses 5–8). Like the "new song" in 5:8–14, the threefold hallel is rendered by heaven and earth.

The heavenly choir again asserts the justice of God's judgment over Babylon whose crime was the murder of the Christian witnesses and the destruction of the earth. The affirmation that God's sentences of judgment are "true and righteous" alludes back to the altar in 16:7, to the announcement of judgment in 11:18, and to the song of Moses and the Lamb in 15:3. Salvation, glory, and power belong to God. These terms should, however, not be spiritualized as referring to the soul but must be understood in their political context. The Roman emperor Augustus was called "savior of the Greeks and of the whole inhabited world," "savior and benefactor," "savior and founder," or "savior and god," whose birthday was the beginning of "good tidings" (gospels). He was the "just and generous lord" whose reign promised peace and happiness, i.e., salvation. The heavenly choir thus asserts: It is not Caesar but God's power and salvation that is revealed in the justice meted out to Babylon/Rome and to its provinces.

The hymn of the great multitude on earth (19:5–8) reminds us of the great eschatological multitude of 7:9 ff and it echoes the "new song" of the Lamb's followers on Mount Sion (14:2 ff). However, the singers are not just the Christians, the servants of God, but all those who have accepted the Gospel that was proclaimed by the angel in 14:6. Those who fear God, the small and the great, are to participate in the praise of God's reign over the earth (verse 5). God's reign and salvation are not oppressive but can be compared with a great wedding feast. The myth of the divine marriage

was widespread in antiquity; and the image of eschatological salvation as a wedding feast was well known
in early Christian tradition (cf. Mt 22:3–14; Lk
14:16 ff; cf. also Mt 26:29 par. and Lk 13:29).

The image of the Church as the bride of Christ is
known especially from the Pauline tradition (Rm
7:2–4; 2 Co 11:2 f; Ep 5:25 ff). However, in Revelation the bride is not the Church but the New Jerusalem
(cf. 21:2,9), the New World of God. The splendor and
glory of this New World are the "righteous deeds" of
the Christians. Not all Christians who were originally
invited but only those who have underwritten this invitation with their righteousness and life will be blessed
and participate in the marriage feast, the symbol for eschatological salvation (cf. Mt 22:11–14). Like the
preceding beatitudes, the fourth blessing is also a warning and promise at the same time. The authentication
"these are the true words of God" does not refer just
to the beatitude but to the whole section (17:1–19:8).

The concluding scene in verse 10 stresses two major
themes of Revelation. The angel is not different from
the prophet because both have the same function,
namely to proclaim the "witness of Jesus." The interpreting angel of apocalyptic literature is here subordi-
nated to Christian prophecy. No one, except God and
the Lamb, may receive the cultic prostration demanded
in the imperial cult. To prostrate oneself (the Greek
word is translated usually with "worship") before the
angel or before the imperial image means to acknowledge their authority, power, and kingship, an acknowl-
edgment due only to God. Therefore, the call to "worship" should not be misunderstood in a depoliticized,
liturgical, pietistic sense. If the author would write
today, he might say: Don't salute the flag, salute God;

or, Don't pledge allegiance to the state, pledge it to God.

STUDY QUESTIONS: What does salvation mean to you? How does your understanding of salvation and worship relate to that of Revelation?

B′. *Eschatological Judgment and Salvation*
Revelation 19:11 to 22:9

The last panel at the top (a) and the climax of the whole book (b) depict the activities of Baby and the reign of Satan (6:7-17; 20:1-3; 21:10). The vision of the New Jerusalem describing the New City of God and the eschatological salvation of the in the new creation (21:1-8).

INTRODUCTION

The final section of Revelation is again composed in the form of an inclusion and intercalation. As we have seen, the visions of 17:1–19:10 are the development and climax of the last plague septet. At the same time they are the first panel (a) in the triptych 17:1–22:9 because they are a part of the "last judgment" scenes (19:11–21:8) told in the central section of the triptych (b). The destruction of the evil forces is thus presented in the reverse order of their introduction. Babylon/Rome which was mentioned last is judged first. This judgment is followed by the punishment of the antichristic/imperial powers through the Parousia Christ (19:11–20). The series of the "last judgments" climaxes in the punishment of the dragon/Satan (20:1–10) and in the destruction of the underworld's powers. The world judgment of all the dead (20:11–14) is followed by the appearance of God's new creation and people (21:1–8).

Babylon/Rome, the antichristic imperial forces, and finally the dragon/Satan are overcome and punished. The last enemies to be judged are the powers of Death and Hades. The New World is a world without any oppressive and dehumanizing powers. God's judgment means salvation for the earth and all of humanity who have not cooperated with evil, destruction, and murder.

The last panel of the triptych (and the climax of the whole book) presents the anti-image of Babylon and the reign of Satan (21:9–22:9a'). The image of the New Jerusalem describes the New City of God and develops the motif of eschatological salvation announced in the praise of 19:1–10.

Revelation 19:11–21:8
PAROUSIA
AND FINAL JUDGMENT

The Parousia of Christ ushers in the day of final judgment. After the three judgment visions of 19:11–21 (cf. verses 11,17,19) announce the punishment of the two beasts with eternal torment and that of their followers with death, three additional judgment visions (cf. 20:1,4,11) describe the punishment of Satan, the reward of the faithful Christians, and the general world judgment. These complete the "last judgment" series that climaxes in the vision of eternal life with God in 21:1–8. This vision is, at the same time, the formal "interlinking joint" to the New Jerusalem visions.

The interpretations of this section vary widely. Especially the vision of the "thousand-year reign," the millennium, has received much scholarly attention. Yet it must be kept in mind that the "last judgment" visions speak about "events" or truth that are beyond space and time. Therefore, this visionary series would be misunderstood if it were understood as presenting a chronological sequence or a description of future events rather than a mythological symbolization of transcendent realities. Since in these visions John refers to the "beyond" of history, he employs traditional mythological language and symbols. The series provides a spectrum of related images for transcendent realities connected with the "last judgment"; its sequence is not chronological but topical, describing the same transcendent truth in its different aspects.

Revelation 19:11–21
THE CONFRONTATION BETWEEN CHRIST AND ANTI-CHRIST

The threefold "and I saw" (19:11,17,19) divides this segment of Revelation into three visions: the appearance of the Parousia Christ (19:11–16), the counterimage of the marriage supper of the Lamb (19:17–18), the punishment of the two beasts and the death of their followers (19:19–21). It seems that after this series of events no living human being is left.

11 And now I saw heaven open, and a white horse appear; its rider was called Faithful and True; he
12 is a judge with integrity, a warrior for justice. ·His eyes were flames of fire, and his head was crowned with many coronets; the name written on him was
13 known only to himself, ·his cloak was soaked in blood. He is known by the name, The Word of
14 God. ·Behind him, dressed in linen of dazzling white, rode the armies of heaven on white horses.
15 From his mouth came a sharp sword to strike the pagans with; he is the one who will rule them with an iron sceptre, and tread out the wine of Al-
16 mighty God's fierce anger. ·On his cloak and on his thigh there was a name written: The King of kings and the Lord of lords.

17 I saw an angel standing in the sun, and he shouted aloud to all the birds that were flying high overhead in the sky, "Come here. Gather to-
18 gether at the great feast that God is giving. ·There will be the flesh of kings for you, and the flesh of great generals and heroes, the flesh of horses and their riders and of all kinds of men, citizens and slaves, small and great."
19 Then I saw the beast, with all the kings of the earth and their armies, gathered together to fight
20 the rider and his army. ·But the beast was taken prisoner, together with the false prophet who had worked miracles on the beast's behalf and by them had deceived all who had been branded with the mark of the beast and worshiped his statue. These two were thrown alive into the fiery lake of burn-
21 ing sulphur. ·All the rest were killed by the sword of the rider, which came out of his mouth, and all the birds were gorged with their flesh.

✠

The following aspects seem to be crucial to the understanding of the passage:

First: Exegetes generally agree that 19:11–16 describes the eschatological return of Christ. Although it is not explicitly stated who the victor on the white horse is, his description repeats features of the introductory vision and section of Revelation (cf. 1:5,14,16; 3:7,14) and thus clearly identifies the figure as Christ. But whereas the message series depicted Christ as the judge in the midst of the Christian community (1:20), 19:11 ff presents him as the judge of the nations and the antagonist of the imperial demonic forces. The Parousia Christ is pictured as a mighty warrior followed by his heavenly army. However, no battle is recorded. He, and not Caesar, is the Great

King who comes to manifest his rule over the nations
(15). As the dragon and beast wore diadems as a sign
of their universal dominion, so Christ wears many diadems that characterize him as the ruler of the world
(19:12). The function of the Divine Warrior-King is to
execute judgment (19:12). Although John stresses that
no one except Christ himself knows his name, he nevertheless mentions three titles: Christ is the "Faithful
and True" who judges with justice (cf. 16:5–7; 19:2).
This title stresses the justice of the divine punishment
and recalls at the same time 3:14 where Christ was
called the faithful and true witness. The justice meted
out by the Parousia Christ proves his faithfulness toward those who have kept "his witness."

The "secret name" indicates that no one can have
power over Christ. The title "The Word of God" seems
to recall the source for John's image in Wisdom
18:15–16: ". . . down from the heavens, from the
royal throne, leapt your all-powerful Word; into the
heart of a doomed land the stern warrior leapt. Carry-
ing your unambiguous command like a sharp sword,
he stood, and filled the universe with death . . ."
The series of names climaxes in the title "King of kings
and Lord of lords" which recalls the title of the Lamb
in 17:14: "Lord of lords and King of kings." The
Parousia means the manifestation of Christ's universal
rulership.

Second: The gory summons of the birds is not descriptive but functions as a warning. The angel in midheaven recalls both the eagle of 8:13 who announced
the three woes and the angel of 14:6 who proclaimed
the eternal Gospel. This hyperbolic announcement of
divine punishment recalls the great day of God's and
the Lamb's wrath proclaimed at the opening of the

sixth seal (6:14–17). Although the image of the "great supper of God" is very repulsive, it is very restrained compared to the scenes of punishment found in later Christian apocalypses.

Third: The last attempt of war on the side of the beast and the pseudoprophet recalls the trumpet interlude of 16:13–16, where the three demonic frogs assembled an army at Armageddon. However, the actual eschatological battle is never described. John seems to use the traditional language of the eschatological war for forensic purposes. The beast and its pseudoprophet, who are the evil powers symbolizing the imperial power and cult, are not killed but taken captive and thrown into the malodorous and very hot fiery lake. It is important to note that their punishment does not encompass that of their human followers who are not thrown in the lake but killed.

STUDY QUESTIONS: Does Revelation justify war with the image of Christ as eschatological warrior? Why did the author transform this traditional apocalyptic image into that of judgment?

Revelation 20:1–15
LIBERATION FROM EVIL
AND UNIVERSAL JUDGMENT

As does the preceding vision, so does 20:1–10 develop
and vary the image of the demonic army. This army
was already presented in the fifth trumpet (9:1–11)
and in the interlude to the bowl visions in 16:13–16.
As in 16:13, so also here the dragon is the chief of the
rebellious forces. The elimination of his power and his
punishment are told in two steps in 20:1–3,7–10. Although the chapter is *formally* divided into three visions and 20:7–10 is formally a part of the vision
beginning in 20:4 ff, *contentually* 20:7–10 is the
conclusion of 20:1–3. The vision of the so-called millennium is thus a part of the second vision, 20:4–10,
and is also an interlude within the overall vision of the
punishment of the ultimate force of evil (20:1–3,
7–10). At the same time, the expressions "first resurrection" and "second death" parallel it with the vision
of the judgment in 20:11–15.

1
20 Then I saw an angel come down from
heaven with the key of the Abyss in his
2 hand and an enormous chain. ·He overpowered

the dragon, that primeval serpent which is the devil and Satan, and chained him up for a thou-

3 sand years. ·He threw him into the Abyss, and shut the entrance and sealed it over him, to make sure he would not deceive the nations again until the thousand years had passed. At the end of that time he must be released, but only for a short while.

4 Then I saw some thrones, and I saw those who are given the power to be judges take their seats on them. I saw the souls of all who had been beheaded for having witnessed for Jesus and for having preached God's word, and those who refused to worship the beast or his statue and would not have the brand-mark on their foreheads or hands; they came to life, and reigned with Christ

5 for a thousand years. ·This is the first resurrection; the rest of the dead did not come to life

6 until the thousand years were over. ·Happy and blessed are those who share in the first resurrection; the second death cannot affect them but they will be priests of God and of Christ and reign with him for a thousand years.

7 When the thousand years are over, Satan will
8 be released from his prison ·and will come out to deceive all the nations in the four quarters of the earth, Gog and Magog, and mobilize them for war. His armies will be as many as the sands of
9 the sea; ·they will come swarming over the entire country and besiege the camp of the saints, which is the city that God loves. But fire will come down
10 on them from heaven and consume them. ·Then the devil, who misled them, will be thrown into the lake of fire and sulphur, where the beast and the false prophet are, and their torture will not stop, day or night, for ever and ever.

11 Then I saw a great white throne and the One who was sitting on it. In his presence, earth and
12 sky vanished, leaving no trace. ·I saw the dead, both great and small, standing in front of his throne, while the book of life was opened, and other books opened which were the record of

what they had done in their lives, by which the dead were judged.

13 The sea gave up all the dead who were in it;
14 Death and Hades were emptied of the dead that were in them; and every one was judged according to the way in which he had lived. Then Death and Hades were thrown into the burning lake.
15 This burning lake is the second death; ·and anybody whose name could not be found written in the book of life was thrown into the burning lake.

✠

The following observations might be helpful for the understanding of this difficult text:

First: After the punishment of the two beasts, the punishment of the dragon is told in two steps: In a first step, the angel, who like the "star" of chapter 9 possesses the key to the abyss, takes the dragon captive, casts him down into the abyss, and seals his prison for a thousand years (20:1-3). The four names of the ultimate evil, "the dragon, the old serpent, the devil, and Satan," refer back to 12:9 when the great dragon together with his angels was cast down to earth. Now the "short while" of his wrath on earth is over, and he is cast down into the underworld. In a second step, the dragon is released from his prison, gathers a ghost army from the four ends of the earth, and marches against the camp of the saints and the beloved city. However, as in 19:19-21, no battle takes place, but fire from heaven devours the army of Gog and Magog so that the devil suffers the same fate as the two beasts. Their punishment and the destruction of all evil demonic power is final and everlasting (20:7-10).

It is debated whether the army of the devil repre-

sents the nations or whether it is a universal army of
the dead. For the latter speaks the fact that at the four
ends of the earth the doors to the underworld were
supposed to be located. Moreover, according to
19:17 f and 21 all human beings are killed. Finally, the
names Gog and Magog are mythical names. They
probably have here a similar meaning as the mythological place Armageddon had in 16:16. The whole vision
thus highlights a different aspect of the same final demonic battle which was also described in 9:1–11;
16:13–16; and 19:19–21. The "events" described in
these visions will not take place in time and space but
belong to the "beyond" of human history. Therefore,
they are told in very ancient mythological language and
imagery.

Second: The victory and punishment over the dragon
is probably told in two steps in order to show that
even during the eschatological assault of the demonic
forces the faithful Christians will be protected. Therefore, the author has sandwiched the vision of the "millennium" (that is, the thousand-year reign of Christ
and the victorious Christians) between the capture and
final assault of the devil and his army. He also has
formally characterized the millennial vision (20:4–6)
and the eschatological assault as one and the same
visionary unit. It is the devil's captivity and not the
reign of the victorious Christians (cf. 22:5) that is
limited to the symbolic time span of a "thousand
years."

If this interpretation of John's compositional intention is correct, then the interlude 20:4–6 has the same
function as the sealing of the 144,000 (7:1–8) or the
measuring of the true worshipers (11:1–2), namely, to
demonstrate the protection of the elect. However,
whereas the previous interludes referred to Christians

living during the endtime, this vision shows the reward
of Christians who were killed. The vision is thus parallel to 6:9–12. Now the number of those who had still
to die is full.

In a vision, 20:4 f announces that those who were
killed because they did not pledge allegiance to the imperial cult now receive justice. The souls of those
Christians who were executed "came to life again" and
assumed rulership together with Christ. The phrase
here does not connote a "spiritual" resurrection because in 2:8 and 13:14 it refers to the resurrection of
Christ or of one of the beast's heads (cf. also Mt 9:18;
Rm 14:9). The vision thus refers to the resurrection of
the Christians who have died in their resistance to the
imperial cult and have remained loyal to God and the
Lamb. Because they have ratified their baptism with
their life-praxis (cf. 1:6; 5:10), they will reign as
priests. Thus John uses here the traditional Jewish expectation of a messianic kingdom in order to stress the
reward of those Christians who have "overcome."
This literary function of the vision 20:4 f is underlined
through the concluding beatitude that those who participate in the first resurrection are exempt from final
judgment and eternal punishment. As priests they will
share in the life-giving ruling power of God and Christ.
They are the "camp of the saints" that is protected from
the last assault of all demonic and evil powers.

Third: The great white throne of the universal judgment scene, 20:11–15, parallels the thrones of 20:4
and recalls the throne room of chapters 4–5. Before
the throne stand all the dead of the whole world and of
all of history. Every human being has the right to receive a just sentence from the Divine Judge. It seems
that John imagines ledgers in which the deeds and life

praxis of the dead are recorded. These ledgers are distinguished from the "book of life" in which the names are recorded of those who have been found "not guilty." Only those who are found guilty are thrown into the "lake of fire." This is the "second death" that the faithful Christians need not fear. Finally, the "last enemy" (cf. 1 Co 15:26) Death, along with his abode Hades, is destroyed. Earth and Heaven of the present creation vanish away in order to make room for the New World of God.

STUDY QUESTIONS: What is the function of the "millennium" vision within the overall composition of Revelation? What is the significance of a universal judgment based on the way people have lived?

Revelation 21:1-8
THE NEW WORLD OF GOD

Revelation's series of messianic judgments reaches its climax in the vision of a new and different world. This vision is at the same time an introduction and exposition of the following section describing the New Jerusalem. The double vision of the new creation and the New Jerusalem (21:1-2) is followed by an addition alluding to the Exodus motif (21:3-4). This vision of the New World is ratified by God who addresses a promise to the victor and a stern warning to those who are tempted by the ways of the dragon and beast (21:5-8). The conclusion of this vision therefore indicates that John is not interested in predictive descriptions but in prophetic encouragement and exhortation.

21 [1] Then I saw a new heaven and a new earth; the first heaven and the first earth had disappeared now, and there was no longer any sea. [2] I saw the holy city, and the new Jerusalem, coming down from God out of heaven, as beautiful as [3] a bride all dressed for her husband. ·Then I heard a loud voice call from the throne, "You see this city? Here God lives among men. He will make his home among them; they shall be his people, and he will be their God; his name is God-with-

4 them. ·He will wipe away all tears from their eyes; there will be no more death, and no more mourning or sadness. The world of the past has gone."

5 Then the One sitting on the throne spoke: "Now I am making the whole of creation new" he said. "Write this: that what I am saying is sure

6 and will come true." ·And then he said, "It is already done. I am the Alpha and the Omega, the Beginning and the End. I will give water from the

7 well of life free to anybody who is thirsty; ·it is the rightful inheritance of the one who proves victorious; and I will be his God and he a son to

8 me. ·But the legacy for cowards, for those who break their word, or worship obscenities, for murderers and fornicators, and for fortune-tellers, idolaters or any other sort of liars, is the second death in the burning lake of sulphur."

✠

The "first" heaven and earth now belong to the past. They were defined by the antagonistic dualism between the dominion of God and Christ in heaven and that of the Dragon and his allies on earth and in the underworld. The Christians are persecuted and embattled because they are the claimants of God's kingdom on earth and the opponents of the dominion of Babylon/Rome. The "new heaven and earth" stand in continuity with the former heaven and earth but form a new unified world characterized by the divine presence among the peoples of God. The New Jerusalem arrayed in the splendor of the "righteous deeds of the saints" is the symbol of God's eschatological salvation and presence. It will come down to earth. John does not envision as Paul did that at the Last Day the Christians "shall be caught up" in the clouds to meet their Lord (cf. 1 Th 4:17), nor does he hope as Daniel did

that the righteous shall shine like stars in heaven (cf.
Dn 12:3 f).

The center of the theological vision and the compositional movement of Revelation is the earth. This new
earth is different from the earth as we know it in that
"heaven will be on earth." Christ's and God's rule and
power cannot coexist with the dehumanizing powers
that corrupt and devastate the earth (19:2). The out-
cries of the persecuted for justice and judgment are
therefore also on behalf of the earth as God's creation.
God's justice and judgment mean not only vindication
of the persecuted and murdered but coincide with
total human well-being and salvation. Not suffering,
weeping, mourning, hunger, captivity, and death but
life, light, and happiness are the realities of the "new
heaven and earth" (cf. also 7:9–15). Therefore, the
sea as the place of the beast and symbol of evil (cf.
13:1) no longer exists (21:1).

A word of God ratifies this vision identifying eschatological salvation as the nonoppressive, liberating
presence of God, whose name is Emmanuel, i.e., God-
with-us. As in 1:8, so here too God's name is "Alpha
and Omega." It is God who makes everything new.
The vision of eschatological salvation concludes with a
promise and a warning. Those who will remain victorious (cf. the promises to the victor in chapters 2–3) will
be the heirs of God's new world. Those who participate
in the destructive praxis of the antidivine oppressive
powers will suffer the second death of eternal punishment. The catalogue of vices (cf. 22:15) is not predictive or descriptive but exhortative. It highlights the various ways of participating in the treason against God's
kingdom. The cowards lose courage in the struggle
with the antidivine forces, the faithless and polluted become the followers of Babylon, the murderers become

the beast's agents in killing those who resist his power, the fornicators, sorcerers, and idolaters worship the powers that destroy the earth, and finally the liars commit themselves to the fundamental and ultimate falsity that breeds violence. All these vices are not abstract and generalized moral failures but behavior related to the betrayal of God's world and power.

STUDY QUESTIONS: How does this vision of human wholeness and salvation change your general understanding of salvation? Is this a vision of "pie in the sky" or does it give theological impulses for Christian praxis?

Revelation 21:9–22:9
THE NEW CITY OF GOD

This last series of visions magnificently elaborates the announcement of eschatological salvation in 21:1–8. It is designed as the third panel in the triptych 17:1–22:9 insofar as it, like the Babylon visions, is introduced by one of the seven bowl angels and is concluded with a dialogue between the angel and the seer. The New Jerusalem is thus formally characterized as the anti-image of the great city Babylon/Rome. Revelation contrasts the splendor and power of the Roman empire with that of the empire of God and Christ in order to encourage its readers to resist the murderous power of Rome. Therefore, this series of visions continues to picture the fulfillment of the promises given to the victor at the end of the seven messages.

In his introductory verses John again stresses that the New Jerusalem comes down from heaven containing within it the glory of God. After the city is described in all its splendor (21:11–14), its measurements are detailed (21:15–21) and its paradise-like life is depicted (21:22–22:3). The whole section climaxes in the vision of the eternal reign of God's high-priestly servants (22:4–5).

9   One of the seven angels that had the seven
bowls full of the seven last plagues came to speak
to me, and said, "Come here and I will show you
10 the bride that the Lamb has married." ·In the
spirit, he took me to the top of an enormous high
mountain and showed me Jerusalem, the holy city,
11 coming down from God out of heaven. ·It had
all the radiant glory of God and glittered like
some precious jewel of crystal-clear diamond.
12 The walls of it were of a great height, and had
twelve gates; at each of the twelve gates there
was an angel, and over the gates were written the
13 names of the twelve tribes of Israel; ·on the east
there were three gates, on the north three gates,
on the south three gates, and on the west three
14 gates. ·The city walls stood on twelve foundation
stones, each one of which bore the name of one
of the twelve apostles of the Lamb.
15   The angel that was speaking to me was carry-
ing a gold measuring rod to measure the city and
16 its gates and wall. ·The plan of the city is perfectly
square, its length the same as its breadth. He
measured the city with his rod and it was twelve
thousand furlongs in length and in breadth, and
17 equal in height. ·He measured its wall, and this
was a hundred and forty-four cubits high—the
18 angel was using the ordinary cubit. ·The wall was
built of diamond, and the city of pure gold, like
19 polished glass. ·The foundations of the city wall
were faced with all kinds of precious stone: the
first with diamond, the second lapis lazuli, the
20 third turquoise, the fourth crystal, ·the fifth agate,
the sixth ruby, the seventh gold quartz, the eighth
malachite, the ninth topaz, the tenth emerald, the
21 eleventh sapphire and the twelfth amethyst. ·The
twelve gates were twelve pearls, each gate being
made of a single pearl, and the main street of the
22 city was pure gold, transparent as glass. ·I saw

that there was no temple in the city since the Lord God Almighty and the Lamb were themselves the
23 temple, ·and the city did not need the sun or the moon for light, since it was lit by the radiant glory of God and the Lamb was a lighted torch
24 for it. ·The pagan nations will live by its light and the kings of the earth will bring it their treasures.
25 The gates of it will never be shut by day—and
26 there will be no night there—·and the nations will come, bringing their treasure and their wealth.
27 Nothing unclean may come into it: no one who does what is loathsome or false, but only those who are listed in the Lamb's book of life.

1 22 Then the angel showed me the river of life, rising from the throne of God and of the
2 Lamb and flowing crystal-clear ·down the middle of the city street. On either side of the river were the trees of life, which bear twelve crops of fruit in a year, one in each month, and the leaves of which are the cure for the pagans.

3   The ban will be lifted. The throne of God and of the Lamb will be in its place in the city; his
4 servants will worship him, ·they will see him face to face, and his name will be written on their fore-
5 heads. ·It will never be night again and they will not need lamplight or sunlight, because the Lord God will be shining on them. They will reign for ever and ever.

6   The angel said to me, "All that you have writ-ten is sure and will come true: the Lord God who gives the spirit to the prophets has sent his angel to reveal to his servants what is soon to take place.
7 Very soon now, I shall be with you again." Happy are those who treasure the prophetic message of this book.

8   I, John, am the one who heard and saw these things. When I had heard and seen them all, I knelt at the feet of the angel who had shown them
9 to me, to worship him; ·but he said, "Don't do that: I am a servant just like you and like your brothers the prophets and like those who treasure

what you have written in this book. It is God that
you must worship."

✠

As are the visions of chapter 20, so is the Jerusalem
vision inspired by Ezekiel 37–48. However, John does
not only expand the material derived from Ezekiel 40 ff
with features from Isaiah 60 ff. He also seems to model
his description of the New Jerusalem after a description of the historical city Babylon, known to us from
the Greek historiographer Herodotus, insofar as he
says that the city stands "a foursquare" and gives its
size in "furlongs" measurements that are also found in
Herodotus' text. It is possible that John's readers
would have perceived that he patterned his Jerusalem
description after that of the historic Babylon.

However, John has molded his traditional materials
in such a way that they express his own vision of future
salvation. First, he has elaborated not only on the size
but also on the overall description of the wall surrounding Jerusalem which has received only scant attention by Ezekiel. Second, John does not describe the
temple but the city, whereas Ezekiel focuses on the description of the new temple. Finally, John stresses that
the throne of God and the Lamb are the center of the
New Jerusalem. Thus the overall vision of the city of
God gathers the main theological motifs and the various visions of eschatological salvation together into a
final focal vision.

First: The city and the wall around the city are
clearly distinguished. Whereas the city seems to be the
universal cosmic symbol of salvation, the wall is clearly
characterized as the symbol of the Church. On the

twelve gates are inscribed the names of the twelve
tribes of Israel (cf. 7:1–8). Moreover, the wall rests
on foundation stones which have on them the names of
the twelve apostles of Christ. Finally, these foundation
stones resemble those which have adorned the breastplate of the Jewish high priest. Thus the wall of the city
seems to be a symbol for the new Israel, the high-
priestly people (cf. 22:4 f) of God, the Church that, according to Christian tradition, was founded upon the
twelve apostles (cf. Ep 2:20). Not the city itself but
only the wall surrounding it symbolizes the eschatological Church.

This distinction between wall and city helps us to
understand the curious measurements with which the
seer describes their relationship. There is an enormous
discrepancy between the size of the city and the size of
the wall. Whereas the size of the city is approximately
1,200 miles, that of the wall is about 144 feet. The
enormous difference in proportion indicates that the
universal cosmic salvation by far exceeds that pre-
figured in the Church. The cosmic universal dimensions of the new city of God are intermingled with
paradisiacal features of the new creation. Not only the
faithful Christians but all those whose names were
registered in the book of life at the final judgment, according to their works, will share in its glory, splendor,
and eternal life.

Second: While the visions of Ezekiel center on the
description of the new temple, Revelation states flatly
that no temple will be found in the city of God. At first
glance, this statement seems to run counter to all Jewish eschatological hopes which John usually cherishes
very much. However, it must not be forgotten that the
whole city has the form of a perfect cube and thus is

characterized as the Holy of Holies (cf. also 21:3). The sacred symbol has now given way to the reality of God's presence.

Therefore, the "servants of God" can be characterized as high priests who have the name of God on their foreheads. But whereas the Jewish high priest had the privilege of entering the Holy of Holies (1 K 6:20) once a year, they will be in the presence of God forever. Like Moses they will see God face to face (22:4 f). According to 1:6 and 5:10, in their baptism the Christians were appointed priests for God. Also, 22:4 f promises that those who ratify their redemption with their life-praxis will exercise their priestly right to live in the presence of God (cf. 7:15 f).

Third: The center of the new city of God is the throne of God, the symbol of imperial power and sovereignty. Not only the Church but all the nations will be the peoples of God (21:3; cf. 15:3). Just as the world-city Babylon/Rome represented the Roman empire and gathered in its precincts the political power and commercial wealth of the nations and of their rulers, so too the New Jerusalem will contain the nations' power and splendor. But whereas Babylon/Rome misused its power and wealth for destroying and corrupting the earth, the vision of God's universal empire promises new life, health, and happiness. The throne—the symbol of God's power—is the source of eternal life (22:1–3).

Within this universal empire of God symbolized by the New Jerusalem the Christians who have remained faithful will live as ruling emperors forever (22:5). The promises of 3:21 and 5:10 are now fulfilled. Nothing will endanger their participatory reign and sovereignty (cf. 20:4–6). However, it is important to stress that the empire and power of God, of Christ, and of the victors are not oppressive and dehumanizing. Life, light, wealth, health, and eternity characterize it. Although Revelation 2:27 had promised that the victors will share in Christ's ruling power over the nations, nowhere does Revelation mention the serfs and subjects of this reign. The empire of God does not spell oppressive rulership but a share in the life-giving and life-sustaining power of God.

STUDY QUESTIONS: Why is this vision of eschatological salvation the key that opens up the theological perspective of Revelation? How does Revelation's vision of the empire of God compare with that announced in the preaching of Jesus?

A′. *Epilogue and Epistolary Frame*
Revelation 22:10 to 22:21

INTRODUCTION

The last verses of Revelation seem to represent a collection of very loosely related sayings. Thus the whole epilogue makes a very disjointed impression. Yet it is clear that verses 8–9 are parallel to 19:10 and are therefore the proper conclusion of the third panel which was introduced in 21:9. At the same time, the emphatic "I John" refers the hearer back to the prologue. Revelation 22:6f seems both to elaborate 21:5b–8 and also to allude to 1:1ff, 3:14, and 19:9b. Therefore, 22:6–9 appears to be a compositional "joint" that interlinks the last series of visions with the epilogue.

It is usually assumed that the speaker of verse 6, "and he said to me," is the bowl angel who showed John the New Jerusalem. However, in verse 7 the speaker is clearly Christ himself. Therefore, it is more likely that in 22:6f as well as in 22:10f the speaker is Christ and not the angel. Then 22:6–20 is a series of revelatory sayings and oracles pronounced by the resurrected Lord. Only 22:8f,17 and 21 are sayings not attributed to Christ.

Revelation 22:21 clearly is the formal conclusion of the open pastoral letter which was introduced in 1:4f. Just as the epistolary introduction alluded to the traditional Pauline letter form, so too does the conclusion.

The conclusion of Revelation is very similar to 1 Corinthians 16:22–24. After a conditional formula of sacral law introduced with "if anyone . . ." (cf. 1 Co 16:22 and Rv 22:18 f) follows an anathema or curse, which in turn is followed by the prayer Marana tha (1 Co 22; Did 10:6) or "come Lord Jesus" that was a part of the eucharistic liturgy. As 1 Corinthians 16:23 f concludes with the wish of grace so too does Revelation 22:21.

10 This, too, he said to me, "Do not keep the prophecies in this book a secret, because the Time is close. ·Meanwhile let the sinner go on sinning, and the unclean continue to be unclean; let those who do good go on doing good, and those who are holy continue to be holy. ·Very soon now, I shall be with you again, bringing the reward to be given to every man according to what he deserves. I am the Alpha and the Omega, the First and the Last, the Beginning and the End. ·Happy are those who will have washed their robes clean, so that they will have the right to feed on the tree of life and can come through the gates into the city. These others must stay outside: dogs, fortune-tellers, and fornicators, and murderers, and idolaters, and everyone of false speech and false life."

16 I, Jesus, have sent my angel to make these revelations to you for the sake of the churches. I am of David's line, the root of David and the bright star of the morning.

17 The Spirit and the Bride say, "Come." Let everyone who listens answer, "Come." Then let all who are thirsty come: all who want it may have the water of life, and have it free.

18 This is my solemn warning to all who hear the prophecies in this book: if anyone adds anything to them, God will add to him every plague men-

19 tioned in the book; ·if anyone cuts anything out
of the prophecies in this book, God will cut off
his share of the tree of life and of the holy city,
which are described in the book.
20   The one who guarantees these revelations repeats his promise: I shall indeed be with you soon.
Amen; come, Lord Jesus.
21   May the grace of the Lord Jesus be with you
all. Amen.

✠

The epilogue, by its content, seems to serve three
functions:

First: It hammers home that the time until the end is
very short and that the Lord will soon return again.
This is stressed here four times (verses 6,7b,12,20)
while it is only found three times in the rest of the
book (cf. 1:1; 2:16; 3:11). Because of this pressing
imminent expectation, John is told not to seal the book
(verse 10) while Daniel had to shut up the words of
his prophecy "until the time of the end" (Dn 12:4).
However, the imminent expectation of Revelation is
not oriented toward the Day of Judgment but to the eschatological coming of Christ who is characterized in
terms of the Davidic Messiah (verse 16; cf. 5:5; Nm
24:17). At the same time he is compared with the
"morning star," the star of Venus, which was the sign
of sovereignty and victory over the nations. Like God
(cf. 1:8; 21:3), Christ is the beginning and the end
(cf. also 1:17; 2:8). The Spirit, the Bride, and those
who hear the words of the prophecy respond to the announcement of Christ's near Parousia with the outcry
and prayer: Come, Come Lord Jesus.

Second: The epilogue drives home that the book's

intention is neither historical and eschatological description nor future prediction but prophetic exhortation and interpretation. Two of the seven beatitudes are found in this section (22:7; cf. 1:3; 22:14; cf. 7:14; 16:15), the list of vices found in 21:8 is repeated almost verbatim (22:15) and a prophetic oracle of impenitence and righteousness (22:10 f) is pronounced. At the same time it is emphasized that the speedy coming of Christ will reward everyone according to their life-praxis (22:12; cf. 20:13; Rm 2:6; 1 P 1:17). The urgency of Revelation's imminent expectation serves hortatory functions.

Third: The last purpose of this lengthy epilogue is prophetic authentication. John stresses again and again that it is Christ who witnesses and guarantees the content of his prophecy (22:16,18). John therefore concludes his book with a solemn declaration of blessing and curse (22:18 f; cf. Dt 4:1 ff). Although this solemn declaration seems to reflect a liturgical and apocalyptic theological convention of the time, it nevertheless indicates that John found it necessary to stress the authority of his prophecy. Probably because of the rival prophetic theology of the Nicolaitans, John had to stress the authenticity of his own prophecy (cf. 1:3; 22:6,9–10,18–19), which can claim a fourfold inspiration: It is authenticated by God, Christ, the Spirit(s), and the apocalyptic angel of revelation (cf. 1:1–3; 22:6,8 f,16,18).

STUDY QUESTIONS: Why does John need to authenticate his prophetic book? Do you think he convinced his prophetic rivals? How would they have answered?

GLOSSARY

Apocalyptic is derived from the Greek word *apok-alypsis/apokalyptein* that means uncovering, disclosure, unveiling, revelation. The expression can, *first,* designate a type of literature written between 200 B.C.E. and 200 A.D.C.E. pertaining to the endtime or to heavenly secrets and realities. *Second,* it can refer to a religious-theological perspective or frame of mind focusing on the urgent expectation of the endtime as the context of God's judging and saving activity for the whole world and for the individual. *Finally,* it can refer to a religious-sociological movement rooted in a group experience of alienation and oppression.

Eschatology: means literally the teaching about the "last" (temporal) or the "ultimate" things and events. The term was first used by scholars of the nineteenth century to label that section of theology which speaks about the doctrines of the individual's physical death, the intermediate state of the soul, the bodily resurrection of the dead, the end of the world and of history.

Parousia: The term is usually used with reference to

Christ's second coming or messianic advent at
the end of this age.

Inclusion: A literary device of marking as well as introducing and ending a literary unit by repeating
words, phrases, symbols, forms, or materials
that signify the author's intent of beginning and
ending a literary unit in a similar way (ABA').

Interlude: The author inserts or sandwiches visions and
auditions of eschatological protection and salvation into a sequence or cycle of apocalyptic
visions that interrupt the pattern of continuous
narrative or temporal progression.

Intercalation: The author employs the literary device of
the double interlude in order to *interlock* or *interlace* different sections of the narrative with
each other (ABA'B'A'').

Mythological Symbolization: A set of images or symbols which as a literary body constitutes a myth
having meaning in itself. It can be broken down
into its component mythological images and
symbols.

APPENDIX

OUTLINE

A. Prologue and Epistolary Frame
   1:1–8

   Title 1:1–3
   Greeting 1:4–6
   Motto 1:7–8

B. The Community under Judgment
   1:9–3:22

   Author and Situation 1:9–10
   Inaugural Vision 1:11–20
   1) Censure and Encouragement 2:1–3:22
      (Seven Messages)

C. God's and Christ's Reign
   4:1–9:21; 11:14–19

   Heavenly Court 4:1–5:14
   2) Seven Seals 6:1–8:1
   3) Seven Trumpets 8:2–9:21; 11:14–19

D. The Community and Its Oppressors
   10:1–11:13; 12:1–15:4
   Prophetic Commissioning 10:1–11:13
   Enemies of the Community 12:1–14:5
   Eschatological Harvest and Liberation 14:6–20; 15:2–4

C'. Judgment of Babylon/Rome
   15:1.5–19:10
   4) Seven Bowls 15:1.5–16:21
   Rome and Its Power 17:1–18
   Judgment of Rome 18:1–19:10

B'. Final Judgment and Salvation
   19:11–22:9
   Parousia and Judgment 19:11–20:15
   The New World of God 21:1–8
   The New City of God 21:9–22:9

A'. Epilogue and Epistolary Frame
   Revelatory Sayings 22:10–17
   Epistolary Conclusion 22:18–21

(Arabic numbers designate seven series)

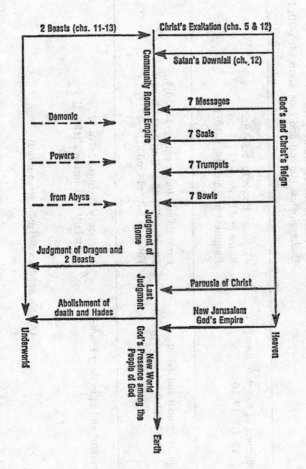

MOVEMENT OF DRAMATIC ACTION IN REVELATION

2 Beasts (chs. 11-13)　　Christ's Exaltation (chs. 5 & 12)

Satan's Downfall (ch. 12)

7 Messages

Demonic

7 Seals

Powers

7 Trumpets

from Abyss

7 Bowls

Community Roman Empire

Judgment of Rome

God's and Christ's Reign

Judgment of Dragon and 2 Beasts

Parousia of Christ

Last Judgment

Abolishment of death and Hades

New Jerusalem God's Empire

Underworld

New World God's Presence among the People of God

Heaven

Earth

SUGGESTED FURTHER READING

FOR FURTHER STUDY

For a more extensive general introduction and theological discussion, see my own contributions:

The Apocalypse (Chicago: Franciscan Herald Press, 1976) Fuller/Sloyan, Krodel, Danker, Schüssler Fiorenza, *Hebrews, James, 1 and 2 Peter, Jude, Revelation* Proclamation Commentaries (Philadelphia: Fortress Press, 1977).

Priester für Gott. Studien zum Herrschafts-und Priestermotiv in der Apokalypse (NTA 7; Münster: Aschendorff, 1972) for an extensive scholarly discussion.

GENERAL INTRODUCTIONS AND COMMENTARIES

For a more general introduction to Jewish apocalypticism, see especially:

W. Schmithals, *The Apocalyptic Movement: Introduction and Interpretation* (Nashville: Abingdon, 1975). The book does not only discuss the literature and phenomenon of Jewish and early Christian apocalypticism but also its theological-religious perspective.

A more scholarly introduction to interpretative-historical problems in Apocalyptic studies is found in the various contributions to the special issue of the *Catholic Biblical Quarterly* (39:3; July 1977) on "Apocalyptic Literature."

The Book of Revelation:

J. L. D'Aragon, "The Apocalypse," in Brown/Fitzmyer/Murphy (eds) *The Jerome Biblical Commentary* (Englewood Cliffs, N.J.: Prentice Hall, 1968) vol. II, pp. 467–93.
A concise introduction to Revelation reviewing and discussing introductory questions and scholarly contributions to the interpretation of the book.

A. Yarbro Collins, *The Apocalypse* (NT Messages 22; Wilmington: Michael Glazier, 1979).
This commentary written for the general public provides excellent historical-literary analyses. However, its "spiritualizing" theological interpretation tends to depoliticize and moralize the theological perspective of the book.

P. S. Minear, *I Saw a New Earth* (Washington: Corpus Books, 1968).
This work provides excellent analyses of Revelation's literary style and imagery, poses questions for pastoral reflection and further study, and concludes by discussing significant problems of theological and literary interpretation. A last section provides an annotated translation of the book as a

literary unit. However, it must be pointed out that Minear's metaphysical interpretation as well as his thesis that the "dwellers and kings of the earth" are faithless Christians led by their false prophets is not widely accepted by scholars today.

R. H. Mounce, *The Book of Revelation* (NICNT; Eerdmans, 1977).
This commentary is a product of conservative New Testament scholarship. The author dialogues not only with major recent scholarly interpretations of Revelation but also with the interpretation of the book in the American Evangelical tradition. Therefore, the work provides much valuable information but must be read critically.

J. J. Pilch, *What Are They Saying About the Book of Revelation?* (New York: Paulist Press, 1978).
This is a popular but very helpful orientation in contemporary scholarship on Revelation. The author not only addresses the general understanding of Revelation as a predictive account of imminent doom but also reviews the liturgical use of the book.